HERBS

Marshall Cavendish

CREDITS
Editor: *Magda Ironside Wood*
Text: *Cynthia Wickham*
Art Editor: *Amelia Edwards*
Picture Stylist: *Heather Standring*
Illustrator: *Sue Richards*

Photographs:
Angel Studio: pages 32 (top), 33
Steve Bicknell: pages 12/13, 18 (top left and
bottom right), 22, 27, 29, 37, 43, 45, 46, 47, 48/9,
50/1
Bodleian Library: page 55
Michael Boys: page 14
Camera Press: page 25
Colonial Williamsburg: pages 16/17
Anthony Denney: pages 13 (inset), 18 (top right
and bottom left), 32 (bottom left and right), 34,
39
Giraudon: page 59 (bottom)
The Three Graces: Raphael/Musee Condee
Mansell Collection: pages 11, 60
Mary Evans Picture Library: pages 56, 57, 61, 62
National Portrait Gallery, London: page 63
(bottom right)
Snark: page 59 (top)
The Rape of Helen by Paris: School of Fra
Angelico/National Gallery, London
Transworld: page 33 (inset)
Michael Wickham: page 14 (right top, centre
and bottom)

Accessories and Services:
herbs from The Old Rectory Herb Garden,
Ightham, Kent
face creams: Culpeper
page 18:
stainless steel tiles: Selfridges
glass bottles: Habitat
page 27:
vinegar dispenser: The Victoria Trading Co.,
1 Camden Walk, London N.1
page 29:
punch bowl: H. Burketts, 3 The Galleries,
Camden Passage, London N.1
page 37:
mirror: The Victoria Trading Co.
page 46 and 47:
wash basin and fittings and bath by Bonsack
Bath Boutique, 14 Mount Street, London W.1
pages 44-53:
authentication: Edward James and Doreen
Jarvis, Holland and Barrat, 19 Goodge Street,
London W.1

Herb plants and seeds are available from
E. & A. Evetts, Ashfields Herb Nursery,
Hinstock, Market Drayton, Shropshire.
Plants cannot be exported. But they have a
special list of seeds for export and welcome
enquiries from countries which permit their
import. Before writing to them notify your
Department of Agriculture, listing the seeds
you wish to import and asking for the
regulations.

Culpeper the Herbalists
of 21 Bruton Street, London W.1, are able to
supply most of the dried herbs mentioned and
will be pleased to send all readers a price list/
order form on receipt of a stamped addressed
envelope.

Published by Marshall Cavendish Books Limited,
58 Old Compton Street, London W1V 5PA

© Marshall Cavendish Limited 1973-84

First printing 1975
Second printing 1976
Third printing 1977
Fourth printing 1982
Fifth printing 1984

Printed and bound in Hong Kong by Dai Nippon

ISBN 0 85685 087 X

All weight and measure equivalents are
approximate. Tablespoons and teaspoons are
Standard Spoon measures and are level.
For the purpose of recipe conversion, Standard
British teaspoons and tablespoons are equivalent
to Standard American ones.
Readers please note: Equivalents for American
ingredients are given in the text in square
brackets.

INTRODUCTION

Whether your interest in herbs is gastronomic, cosmetic or mere curiosity, you are bound to enjoy this book. For instance, did you know that fennel mixed with yogurt makes a tingling, skin-nourishing face pack? That tarragon or basil absolutely transforms vinegar? This book tells you why and how.

Begin at the beginning and you'll be amazed at the sheer number and variety of the herbs described in the concise dictionary. The many practical aspects are well illustrated in the following chapter which explains in detail how to obtain your own supply of herbs in the very nicest, most satisfying way—by growing them yourself. (And don't despair if you're a flat-dweller or don't have a garden; herbs can be cultivated in window boxes and pots.)

The chapters on how to use herbs in food and drink form the heart of the book—and, in addition to valuable general information—over 50 mouthwatering recipes, all specially created to encourage you to use herbs imaginatively in your cooking. If the succulent Beef Stew doesn't use up all your rosemary, you could use some in an infusion to condition and darken your hair if you're a brunette. This is only one of so many useful ideas in the 'Herbs for Beauty' section, where you'll find guides to how to make your own beauty products inexpensively. And that's not the end of the versatility of herbs, for if you've any to spare they can be put into the charming and easy-to-make pot pourris and sachets illustrated in 'Gifts to Make with Herbs'. The book ends with an interesting history of herbs and their sometimes bizarre uses through the ages.

Growing and using herbs is a creative and rewarding pastime. Rediscover herbs—growing them puts you back in touch with Nature and using them brings individuality to your cooking and your home.

CONTENTS

DICTIONARY OF HERBS

A

Alchemilla Vulgaris

Allium Sativum

Allium Schoenoprasum

Anethum Graveolens

Angelica Archangelica

Anthemis Nobilis

Anthriscus Cerefolium

Artemisia Abrotanum

Artemisia Absinthum

Artemisia Dracunculus

Artemisia Vulgaris

Asperula Odorata

B

Borago Officinalis

C

Calendula Officinalis

Carum Petroselinum

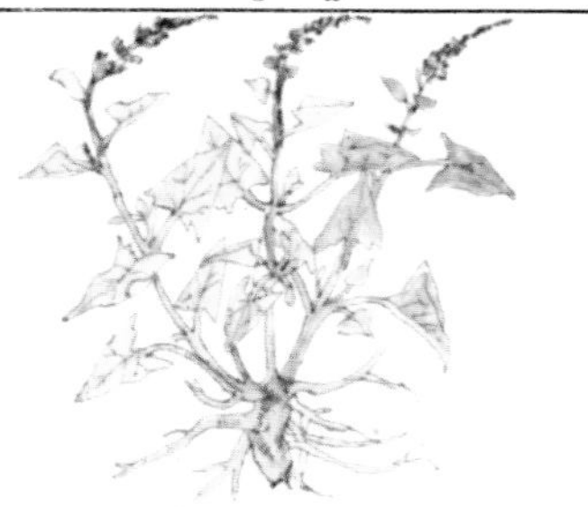

Chenopodium Bonus-Henricus

Coriandrum Sativum

E

Eruca Sativa

F

Foeniculum Vulgare

H

Helianthus Annuus

Hyssopus Officinalis

I

Inula Helenium

L

Laurus Nobilis

Lavandula Officinalis

Ligusticum Officinale

Lippia Citriodora

M

Marrubium Vulgare

Melissa Officinalis

Mentha Piperita

Mentha Rotundifolia

Mentha Spicata

Monarda Didyma

Mentha Pulegium

Myrrhis Odorata

N

Nepeta Cataria

Alchemilla Vulgaris (Lady's Mantle). A hardy perennial plant, Lady's Mantle—although once called the Alchemist's Herb and considered to have almost magical healing properties —is now usually grown for its decorative pale green flowers rather than as a herb. It grows 6-18 inches tall and prefers a moist but well-drained soil.

Allium Sativum (Garlic). Technically a vegetable and not a herb, Garlic is a member of the Lily family and, therefore, related to Onions and Chives. The separate cloves from each bulb are planted in light well-composted soil in a sunny position about 1 inch deep and 6 inches apart in the early spring.
The bulbs can be lifted when the leaves have died down in the late summer then hung up to dry in a dry place.

Allium Schoenoprasum (Chives). This perennial plant produces clumps of mildly onion-flavoured green spears. Chives, which grow to only 4-6 inches, make good edging plants in summer and have pretty mauvey-blue flowers for cutting. Sow in early summer, and thin the seedlings to 1 foot apart. Once established, the clumps of Chives need dividing every four years. They will grow almost anywhere, including in pots on window-sills, and benefit from being cut frequently—which is no problem because once you have Chives, you will use them every day.

Anethum Graveolens (Dill). This is a beautiful feathery herb, growing to $1\frac{1}{2}$-3 feet tall, and is sharply aromatic. It is a hardy annual and has leaves similar to Fennel but blueish-green in colour and more delicate. In late summer it has yellow flowers that look lovely in flower arrangements, and whose seeds are used for pickling cucumbers. Sow the seeds in late spring in well-drained soil in a sunny place and give the plant quite a lot of water. As it is quick-growing from seed it will do well in pots or boxes on a window-sill.

Angelica Archangelica (Angelica). This giant biennial, which grows to 5-6 feet tall, has huge green umbels. The seeds should be sown in autumn—they are only viable directly after the parent plant has shed them—in the bed. If possible plant them in rich damp soil in a fairly shaded position. When the seedlings are a few inches high thin them to 6 inches apart. Germination is slow, but once the plants are established they will seed themselves.

Angelica is difficult to accommodate unless you have a fairly large garden, but it is a beautiful plant, and is also good for cutting for the house.

Anthemis Nobilis (Camomile). Camomile is also called 'The Plant's Physician' because any plant near it will thrive, and it is still grown in herb gardens to keep the other plants well and happy. Above all, however, it is always thought of as a material for fragrant lawns, the stems go along the ground and white daisy-like flowers rise up 12-14 inches. It is these flowers that are dried to make what some people consider the most refreshing teas in the world. The seeds are sown in the late spring, but as it seeds itself as well as spreading, and will grow in any soil if it gets some sun, once it is established you have it for ever.

Anthriscus Cerefolium (Chervil). This is slightly similar in appearance to Parsley but is more delicate and fern-like. It is an annual, grows to about 1 foot, and is quite happy in boxes or pots on a window-sill. Chervil appreciates a shady place, grows best when sown in late summer in well-drained soil and is one of the earliest herbs to be used after the winter. It can be substituted for Parsley or Chives and has a slight aniseed flavour.

Artemisia Abrotanum (Southernwood). This plant is very poisonous and is not to be eaten. Southernwood is a perennial and one of the most beautiful silver-grey foliage plants. It was traditionally grown in herb gardens to keep the witches out, and is still popular in old-fashioned gardens as a decorative plant. The leaves smell pungent and spicy even when uncrushed, and it is popular in cities for window-boxes as it is capable of withstanding dirt and traffic fumes. The plants prefer a sunny position in well-drained soil, and grow 2-4 feet tall. Plant originally in autumn or spring and increase by cuttings.

Artemisia Absinthum (Wormwood). Wormwood, another very beautiful Artemisia, with furry grey leaves, grows into a small shrub 2-3 feet high. It is one of the bitterest herbs, second only to Rue. It is excellent grown in both herb and flower gardens, its silver-grey foliage contrasting well with flowers and green leaves. Wormwood is very easy to grow, thriving in most situations. Plant it in spring. Being a strong growing perennial it sometimes gets straggly, so it needs firmly cutting back in summer to keep it in order.

Artemisia Dracunculus (Tarragon). There are two varieties of Tarragon, both perennial—*Artemisia Dracunculus* which is the true French Tarragon and is the best, and *Artemisia Dracunculoides*, the Russian Tarragon, which has slightly less flavour.
Tarragon can almost never be grown from seed but it can be grown from root divisions or cuttings planted in spring. The French variety will probably not set seed in a temperate climate and is not easy to propagate, but once a well-rooted plant is established it appears to be quite happy and multiplies slowly. The Russian variety is a very strong grower and tends to spread rather like Mint if not controlled. The French variety grows to 2-3 feet tall, the Russian to 3-5 feet. Both like a light soil and a dry sunny position, and can also be grown indoors in a large pot.

Artemisia Vulgaris (Mugwort). This is another perennial member of the lovely Artemisia family. It grows 2-4 feet tall with a woody stem and is usually bought in late spring as a plant. The flower shoots are cut from mid to late summer and the leaves thrown away—it is only the buds which are used as seasoning.

Asperula Odorata syn. Galium Odoratum (Woodruff). When this herb is slightly dry it is very sweet-smelling—the leaves develop a scent like new-mown hay. It grows in clumps about 8 inches high and 14 inches across—so it will cover quite a lot of ground if you want it to— and has white flowers like tiny stars in early summer. Woodruff grows wild in shady places in woods and should be given a similar position in a garden. It is a perennial which is one of the herbs that is very difficult to grow from seed so it is best to buy plants in late spring.

 Borago Officinalis (Borage). This hardy annual plant is happy in the poorest soil. It grows to $1\frac{1}{2}$-$2\frac{1}{2}$ feet tall and has furry, grey-green leaves and brilliant blue star-like flowers, much-loved by bees. Seeds can be sown in early summer and once established it will seed itself happily. The leaves and flowers are used in various drinks.

 Calendula Officinalis (Pot Marigold). Marigolds have been connected with, and grown in, the herb garden from ancient times and are one of the easiest and most rewarding flowers to grow. Their glorious bright orange flowers are a brave and stimulating addition to any garden, window-box or large pot. The plant is an annual, very easily grown from seed, growing to 20 inches high, happy in most situations but revelling in a sunny place. The seeds are sown in early autumn to produce extra large flowers the following year. The Latin name *Calendula* means 'through the months', an apt name as if the dead heads are picked off the flowers go on and on all through the summer. Although the slightly sticky, furry leaves have a spicy scent quite unlike any other, it is the petals which are used in cooking.

Carum Petroselinum syn. *Petroselinum Crispum* (Parsley). You will use a lot of Parsley as there are few dishes it does not improve, so grow plenty of it. Apart from its taste, Parsley, a biennial and another member of the Umbelliferae family, is also full of vitamins, particularly vitamin C. Sow the seeds from spring to mid-summer in drills 1 foot apart, in fairly damp soil in a shady place. Parsley is slow to germinate, but it transplants easily and makes an excellent edging plant. It is also very successful in pots and window-boxes.

Chenopodium Bonus-henricus (Good King Henry or Mercury). This perennial plant, which reaches up to 3 feet tall, is often grown as a substitute for spinach—it resembles it and has all the goodness associated with it. It likes good rich soil and a sunny position. Sow the seeds 1 inch deep in drills 1 foot apart in early summer. After a month thin the seedlings out to 9 inches apart. In autumn cover the bed with a thin layer of manure. The beds should be renewed every 3 or 4 years.

Coriandrum Sativum (Coriander). This attractive feathery annual grows to about 1½ feet and provides both leaves —with a flavour somewhat like dried orange peel—and seeds for the kitchen. Sow the seeds in rich light soil in rows 1 foot apart all through the summer— then you will have a continuing supply of young leaves, and a crop of seeds.

 Eruca Sativa (Rocket). This annual salad plant with pungent tasting leaves is used a great deal in Southern France and Italy. It grows 1-2 feet high and has cream-coloured flowers. It is easily raised from seed and will grow almost anywhere—although it prefers moist, rich soil. Sow the seeds throughout the summer in short rows, and thin

the seedlings out to about 8 inches apart. The leaves will be ready to eat 6-8 weeks after sowing.

 Foeniculum Vulgare (Fennel). Fennel, with its fine feathery foliage and yellow umbels of flowers, grows to 4-6 feet tall and is a decorative garden plant. It is a perennial, but should be transplanted before the tap root has grown too long. A well-established plant does not take very kindly to being moved.

 Helianthus Annuus (Sunflower). The lovely giant Sunflowers have long been associated with herb gardens. The large seeds are sown in spring where the plants are to flower. Sunflowers are not particular about the soil they are in, but they do like sunshine. The great flowers appear in early autumn and grow up to 10 feet tall or more. The oil which forms some 40 per cent of their seeds is an excellent and healthy cooking oil, and both the flower heads and seeds can be used.

Hyssopus Officinalis (Hyssop). This charming little perennial sub-shrub with bright blue, pink or white flowers in the summer, is ideal for borders in the herb garden. It grows 1½-2 feet tall and is hardy and happy in most situations, preferring a sunny place and a light soil. Seeds are sown in spring in drills ¼ inch deep and the seedlings planted out 1-1½ feet apart.

 Inula Helenium (Elecampane). This is a tall, very decorative perennial herb of the daisy family, 4-7 feet tall, with large leaves. In late summer it has shaggy yellow flowers which sometimes measure over 3 inches across. It is grown in the herb garden as a tall background for other herbs. Grow it either from seed or by root division, planting in the spring. Elecampane grows reasonably well in light soils, but prefers fairly rich, well-drained soil and a sunny position.

 Laurus Nobilis (Bay). This is the sweet Bay tree. A mature tree may grow to 12 feet tall or more over 20 years. It has small yellow flowers in spring followed by purplish berries in a warm dry summer. You can grow it from seed

sown in the spring, but this is sometimes difficult to do and it is probably easier to buy it as a small pot plant. Grow it in well-drained soil in a sheltered position or keep it in a pot on a shaded balcony or verandah.

Lavandula Officinalis (Lavender). Most people are familiar with Lavender, with its grey-green needle-like foliage, spears of fragrant flowers and a scent which is, perhaps, the most refreshing in the world. Propagation is easiest by striking green cuttings about mid-summer. Grow in a sunny position in poor soil. Although flower-stems may be removed before winter it is not advisable to trim the bush until any spring frosts are over. Lavender bushes have a lifespan of 5-6 years, after this they should be renewed.

Ligusticum Officinale Syn. Levisticum Officinale (Lovage). Lovage is a giant-sized perennial, growing 5-7 feet high with yellowish flower umbels in late summer. It prefers rich moist soil and is happy remaining in the same ground for a number of years. Either sow the seeds in spring, or propagate by root division in spring or autumn. Both the leaves and seeds are used and are very pungent, being noticeably stronger than other herbs and tasting like a cross between celery and curry.

Lippia Citriodora (Lemon Verbena). This shrubby plant—which is sometimes confused with *Verbena Officinalis* (Vervain or Pigeon's Grass)—can grow to over 10 feet, and has long pointed lemon-scented leaves, and small mauve flowers in late summer. Lemon Verbena was introduced from Chile in 1781 and is not hardy. Grow it from a cutting planted in late spring in light, well-drained soil in a warm, sheltered position. In sheltered places it will probably survive the winter outside. Alternatively, you can grow it in a pot and take it indoors or into the greenhouse if a frosty winter threatens.

 Marrubium Vulgare (White Horehound). This hardy herbaceous perennial, reaching 2 feet tall with round wrinkled leaves, is now grown mainly for its ancient historical associations—it is one of the very oldest medicinal herbs. Grow it from seeds planted in spring in a shady position and dryish soil. Thereafter propagate the plant by root division.

Melissa Officinalis (Lemon Balm). This hardy herbaceous perennial grows 2-4

feet high with light green, deeply veined, heart-shaped leaves strongly scented of lemon, and small whitish flowers. It is easily grown in most soils from seed sown in spring, or can be propagated by root division in spring and autumn. It also seeds itself. Several bushes grown together make a beautiful sweet-smelling hedge.

Mentha sp. (Mints). There are over 40 varieties of Mint, of which a few—all perennial—are well-known and widely grown. Mints cannot be sown by seed. They must be grown from root division —which is no problem as anyone who has Mint is only too glad to get rid of some. It grows well in a sheltered position in moist rich soil and spreads very fast so, ideally, it should be grown on its own with the roots restricted either by planting it in a box plunged in the earth or by driving slates down around it. The most common varieties of Mint, all of them edible, are:

Mentha Piperita (Peppermint). This grows 1-2 feet tall with longish pointed leaves and has purple flowers in autumn. It is the oil from this plant that is used to give the peppermint flavour to confectionery.

Mentha Pulegium (Pennyroyal). This is a tiny creeping Mint, growing to only 4-6 inches tall, with purple flowers in autumn. Like Camomile, it can be used for fragrant lawns.

Mentha Rotundifolia (Apple Mint, Round-leafed Mint). This grows 2-3 feet tall or more, with round furry leaves and has purplish-white flowers in summer. It is often used as a substitute for Spearmint and, once tasted, is usually preferred to it.

Mentha Spicata syn. *Mentha Viridis* (Spearmint, Lamb Mint, Common Green Mint). This is perhaps the best-known variety of Mint and the one generally used for Mint Sauce. It grows 1-2 feet tall with pointed leaves and has purplish flowers in autumn. You can grow it in pots or on a window-sill, but keep the plant pinched down to about 6 inches.

Monarda Didyma (Bergamot, Bee Balm, Oswego Tea). This perennial is one of the most decorative scented herbs, with aromatic foliage and honeysuckle-shaped scarlet flowers. It grows readily from seed, and should be sown in the summer for flowering the following year. It will grow to 2½-5 feet depending upon the soil, and position. In light rich

soil you can grow it in full sun; in hot dry soil it prefers some shade. In dry weather it should be well-watered. Apart from the hybrid varieties of *Monarda Didyma* which are now available—their flowers lavender, purple, or salmon pink—there is also *Monarda Fistulosa* (Wild Bergamot) which has purple flowers and grows to 3-4 feet. Bergamot flowers in late summer and both the flowers and leaves are used.

Myrrhis Odorata (Sweet Cicely). This is an extremely decorative perennial, Umbelliferous plant growing from 2-4 feet high, with fern-like leaves. Like Lovage it is a strong-growing plant which gets bigger every year. Sow the seeds in late spring, if possible in fairly rich, well-drained soil. (It will, however, grow in most places as long as it is not too dry.) Thereafter you can propagate it by root division in early spring. Sweet Cicely is a particularly valuable plant as it is pickable for a great deal of the year, appearing in earliest spring and not departing until early winter. It has white umbels of flowers in spring. It is the leaves and stems which are used, and improve all herb mixtures with their very slight, fresh 'anise' taste.

 Nepeta Cataria (Catmint, Catnip). This perennial grow to 1½-3 feet with roughly heart-shaped leaves and white, lavender or purple flowers during the summer. Grow it in light, well-composted, soil in a sunny position. Sow the seed in spring where the plant is to grow, or propagate by root division from late autumn to early spring.

 Ocimum Basilicum (Basil). Common or Sweet Basil is a half-hardy annual and grows, in good warm conditions to about 1 foot high. It has roughly tri-angular leaves and cream-coloured flowers. A delicate plant, Basil does best of all under glass as it needs heat to bring out its clove-like flavour. Sow the seeds in late spring. If you have no greenhouse give it the sunniest position in the garden or grow it in a pot on a sunny window-sill. When a young plant is established, keep pinching out the top to make it bush out.

Origanum sp. (Marjoram). This perennial is one of the most useful culinary herbs, and one of those that make up a traditional *Bouquet Garni*.
(See page 19).

Origanum Majorana syn. Majorana Hortensis. (Knotted Marjoram). Although a perennial, in temperate climates this must be treated as a half-hardy annual. It is inadvisable to sow it outside until the soil has warmed up, sometimes as late as the end of May. It can be sown earlier in heat and set out in a warm sheltered bed. (If frost threatens protect the plants with cloches.)

Origanum Onites (Pot Marjoram). This is green-stemmed and generally white-flowered. It is particularly useful as it can be grown in a pot indoors for use during the winter.

Origanum Vulgare (Wild Marjoram). This has reddish stems and generally purple flowers. It is indigenous to the limestone hills of Britain, where the temperate climate gives it a similar, but somewhat milder, flavour to that of *Origanum Onites* (Pot Marjoram). When grown in hot climates such as Southern Italy, however, it is known as Oregano and has a pungent taste.

 Portulaca Oleracea (Purslane). This annual only grows to 6 inches high and is a sprawling plant with rosettes of fleshy leaves. Sow the seeds in short rows in spring and throughout the summer in a sunny place in dry, warm soil. Thin the plants to give 6 inches between them. The young leaves are picked as needed and eaten like spinach.

 Rosmarinus Officinalis (Rosemary). This ever-green shrub makes a large sprawling bush 6 feet or more in height with blue-mauve flowers in spring. It should have a reasonably sheltered place in sandy well-drained soil and, although it is hardy, it cannot withstand severe frost. A dry, warm, sunny border suits it best—and if it is happy it can live for 20 years. Seed can be sown in early summer, but Rosemary is more normally grown from rooted cuttings or bought plants. You can also grow it quite easily in a rich loamy soil indoors as long as you keep it well-watered.

Rumex Acetosa (Sorrel). A sort of cross between a herb and a leaf vegetable, Sorrel grows to 2 feet tall with arrow-shaped leaves. It is grown extensively in France for use in Sorrel soup and in salads. Sow the seed in spring, in rows, leaving 12 inches between the plants.

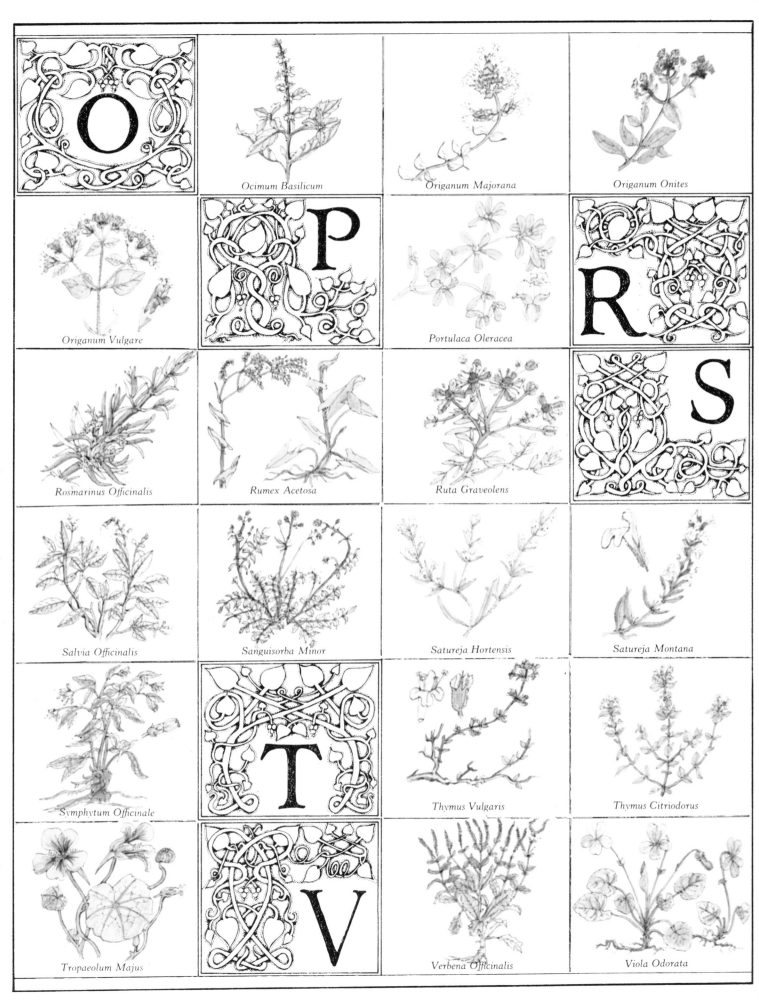

Ocimum Basilicum

Origanum Majorana

Origanum Onites

Origanum Vulgare

Portulaca Oleracea

Rosmarinus Officinalis

Rumex Acetosa

Ruta Graveolens

Salvia Officinalis

Sanguisorba Minor

Satureja Hortensis

Satureja Montana

Symphytum Officinale

Thymus Vulgaris

Thymus Citriodorus

Tropaeolum Majus

Verbena Officinalis

Viola Odorata

Sorrel is a strong growing perennial and once established can be propagated by division of the roots in autumn and spring. It likes a light soil and sunny position. Cut off the flowers to prevent the plant running to seed and becoming tough.

Ruta Graveolens (Rue). This hardy evergreen shrub with lovely little round bluey-green leaves grows to about 2 feet, and has soft yellow flowers in summer. It is now grown almost entirely for its decorative qualities and because of its long historical association with the herb garden. It is quite simple to grow, rooting easily from cuttings and growing in almost any soil. It does, however, prefer a sunny position.

Salvia Officinalis (Sage). This is a little shrub about 2 feet high with narrow greyish-green leaves and spikes of purple flowers. Sage will grow almost anywhere but, like most herbs, is happiest on well-drained soil and needs a warm, sunny position to develop fully its aromatic oils. If growing from seed, sow in early summer in a seed box pricking off the seedlings to a

A sixteenth-century apothecary mixing his herbal potions and medicines.

nursery bed before transferring them to their final position. Sage can also be grown in a pot, or can be increased by root division or cuttings. Renew the plants every three or four years as they get thin and woody.

Sanguisorba Minor syn. Poterium (Salad Burnet). Used in England since the sixteenth century, this perennial herb grows 1½-2 feet and has rosettes of leaves 1½ feet across with pink or white flowers during the summer. It is extremely decorative and ideal in the garden as, in most climates, it manages to produce green leaves all the year round. It is extremely hardy and will grow in most soils, preferring chalky ground. Sow it in rows 1 foot apart in the spring; once established it will seed itself. It is particularly good for growing in window-boxes and pots. For regular use the plant should not be allowed to flower and should be cut back to about 6 inches high. Salad Burnet can be cut again and again so you only need a few plants, but pick just the young leaves: the older ones tend to be tough.

Satureja (Savory). Savory is a very useful aromatic kitchen herb and looks like a long-leafed thyme. Two distinct varieties are grown:

Satureja Hortensis (Summer Savory). This is a little bushy annual which grows to 1½ feet and has pink flowers in late summer. Grow it from seed sown in early summer. You can also grow it in pots indoors throughout the winter.

Satureja Montana (Winter Savory). This hardy dwarf evergreen grows 1-1½ feet tall and is extremely useful for a flavouring in the winter when everything else is dead. As it is a perennial it is perhaps preferable to Summer Savory. Seeds can be sown in a fairly light soil in late spring, giving the plants 6-8 inches between them.

Symphytum Officinale (Comfrey, also known as Knit-bone and Boneset). Comfrey is a perennial, and the biggest and tallest member of the large Borage family. It grows to 4-5 feet tall and has bell-like flowers in purple, pale yellow, or white and large hairy leaves. Comfrey is now mainly grown for its decorative and historical qualities, (the blue flowered variety is particularly pretty). It can be grown from seed sown in the spring or from root cuttings taken in late autumn. Comfrey spreads a bit so it needs room—grow the plants 2 feet apart. It will grow in almost any position, but does like damp soil.

Thymus sp. (Thymes). Thyme—a perennial evergreen—is another of the very popular herbs widely used in *Bouquet garni* and stuffings. Sow plant cuttings in early summer in a sunny, sheltered position in well-drained soil which is not too rich. Replace the plants every three or four years. Thyme can, too, be grown indoors in pots and boxes.

Thymus Vulgaris (Common Thyme). This grows in the shape of a low bush about 1 foot high, and has strongly scented tiny leaves.

Thymus Citriodorus (Lemon Thyme). This is of creeping growth, only 6 inches high and grows well amongst paving stones.

Tropaeolum Majus (Nasturtium). Nasturtiums are such a part of the flower garden—dwarf varieties for bedding and edging, trailers and climbers for covering banks and screens, and every kind in boxes and pots—that it is perhaps a surprise to find them in the herb garden. But the spicy, peppery leaves are very rich in Vitamin C and the fresh flowers are delicious in salads. (The leaves, petals and seeds have long been used in the East for teas and salads.) Nasturtiums are annuals and are extraordinarily easy to grow, although subject to Black Fly. Sow the seeds in late spring where they are to flower. The richer the soil the more the plants will go to leaf.

Verbena Officinalis (Vervain). Vervain is grown in herb gardens mainly because of its ancient magical associations—it was used to ward off evil powers—although in France a tea is still made with it. It is a pretty perennial plant which grows to 1½-2 feet high with pointed leaves and spikes of mauve flowers. Sow seeds in spring where the plant is to grow, thereafter it will seed itself if you let it.

Viola Odorata (Violet, Sweet). This lovely little perennial plant flowers in the spring and only grows to 6 inches tall, so it is ideal for borders. It is sometimes used in tea, but is now mainly grown in herb gardens for its historical associations. Buy it as a plant in spring and give it a semi-shaded position in poor soil. Once established it will increase rapidly either seeding itself or spreading by runners.

growing herbs indoors

If you want to grow herbs but have no garden it is perfectly possible to have some in a window-box or in pots on a window-sill.

Often, too, in order to keep them going longer herbs like *Satureja Hortensis* (Summer Savory) are dug out of the garden in late summer and put in pots in the house. If you have sharp winters, *Mentha* (Mint) should be potted at the same time but left outside until the first frost and then brought in.

Which herbs to grow

The herbs most suitable for a window-box are these low ones which are also content growing in pots:

Allium Schoenoprasum (Chives)
Anthriscus Cerefolium (Chervil)
Carum Petroselinum (Parsley)
Ocimum Basilicum (Basil)
Origanum sp. (Marjoram)
Thymus sp. (Thyme)

The larger herbs—*Borago Officinalis* (Borage), *Foeniculum Vulgare* (Fennel) and *Salvia Officinalis* (Sage)—will be quite happy in pots, too, but they will grow much smaller than in a garden.
Those herbs with wandering root systems—*Artemisia Dracunculus* (Tarragon), *Melissa Officinalis* (Lemon Balm) and *Mentha sp.* (Mint) grow quite happily in pots, but keep them on their own as they will overrun and subdue any bedfellows.

Laurus Nobilis (the Bay Tree) is, of course, traditionally happy in a pot of rich soil.

Where to grow them

A cool room of not more than 60°F. (16°C.) in the day is best for herbs. Put a sun-lover like *Thymus* (Thyme) nearest the window or in full sun outside; *Mentha* (Mint) will be happiest in semi-shade.

Where space is really limited and every corner has its pot, as on a roof garden or a small balcony, herbs which have the same watering requirements—apart from those with wandering root systems —can be successfully grouped together in a large pot.

Soil

The soil for herbs in pots is very important, get a special bag of soil from a nursery or gardening shop, stating what you want it for. A good potting compost for herbs is one made up of equal parts of sand, leaf mould and soil.

Planting

Most herbs can be grown in pots following the method you would use to grow them in the garden.

Allium Schoenoprasum (Chives) can be sown as seed in the pot in which it is to live, the 'grass' will come up within a few weeks.

Carum Petroselinum (Parsley) seeds should be soaked overnight in hot water before sowing.

Anethum Graveolens (Dill), *Thymus sp.* (Thyme), *Ocimum Basilicum* (Basil) and *Origanum sp.* (Marjoram) should be sown in a seed box in moist soil and covered with glass, or put in a propagating box. When the seedlings are about 2 inches high and easy to handle they can be transplanted to their final quarters.

Care

Like all house plants, herbs in pots indoors like an undisturbed, even temperature, and regular watering.
If the plants are inside all the time they must be given an airing from time to time. If possible, put them by an open window in the sun.
Herbs living indoors also need humidity. Stand the pots on a bed of gravel or pebbles in a trough or saucer and keep water in the saucer—below the top of the pebbles so that the plants do not have wet feet. The water in the saucer will evaporate, and a moist atmosphere rise around the plant.
Finally, remember that sudden changes of temperature and draughts are as fatal to herbs as they are to the most exotic house plant.

Herbs growing in a window-box, or a pot of Basil on a kitchen ledge (inset), can be both decorative and useful.

herb gardens

Herbs are enjoying a great revival, and it would be nice if herb gardens were to as well. They need not be large, but they should be enclosed, or in a sheltered position and the plants spaced out. The whole thing could have a simple formality reminiscent of monastery courtyard gardens. Herb gardens are very pleasant to walk through, occasionally picking a leaf and crushing it to release its perfume. And on hot days the aromatic scent of the herbs will drift through the whole garden.

Planning a herb garden

Any herb garden, whether it is a simple border or a complicated Knot Garden (see endpapers for suggested plans), needs careful thought. You must know about the heights and growing habits of the plants (see dictionary) otherwise your tall subjects may be planted in the front of the bed or next to, and smothering, the short or creeping herbs. And beware planting *Artemisia Dracunculus* (Tarragon) and *Mentha* (Mint) in a mixed bed—they tend to take over, strangling everything else. Try to keep them separate, or put slates down into the soil to stop their roots from creeping over into the rest of the bed.

When planning a garden think too about which herbs like sun and which are happier in dappled shade. Generally speaking *Origanum* (Marjoram), *Rosmarinus Officinalis* (Rosemary), *Salvia Officinalis* (Sage) and *Thymus* (Thyme), (which all come from the dry Mediterranean hills), need a lot of sun and can stand dryness, while the juicier green herbs such as *Allium Schoenoprasum* (Chives), *Anthricus Cerefolium* (Chervil), and *Mentha* (Mint) prefer a moist spot and some shade.

Paths and divisions

Herb gardens must look neat, and you need to be able to reach each plant to pick it, so the larger gardens are usually divided into small plots by stone, brick

A well-tended herb garden will look attractive whatever its form: formal (top left), rustic (centre and bottom left) or just a simple plot (far left).

or gravel paths. Or, alternatively, you could have fragrant paths of creeping *Thymus* (Thyme) or *Mentha Pulegium* (Pennyroyal).

Divisions between some of the herbs are a good idea, too, as they stop the plants getting mixed up together. These, again, can be of brick or stone. Or you could have hedges of *Lavandula Officinalis* (Lavender) but be warned, they need constant care and clipping to keep them neat.

Situation

Most herbs came originally from the sunny Mediterranean countries, where they grow in dry, poor and sometimes rocky soil. So choose a sheltered, sunny, south-facing plot for your herb garden, and make sure that the soil is well-drained. Herbs will usually grow in any soil—as long as it is not really heavy. If possible it is a good idea to have the ground sloping slightly towards the south. Then herbs that need sun can be planted at the top, and those that need a damper, shadier spot can be put in the bottom.

What to grow

This is, of course, really a question of personal taste and the size of the proposed herb garden. A small selection of the better known herbs, both annuals and perennials, will give you a useful stock for cooking.

Preparing the bed

The better prepared the bed is, the better the garden will be. The soil, of whatever type, should be well dug, forked over, given a final raking and firmed. Do all this in early autumn and then give the bed a final dig over in spring.

Growing from seed

Some herbs, the annuals and those which will self-seed but for the purposes of cultivation are treated as annuals, are freshly grown from seed each spring.

Sow the seeds as soon as the danger of frost is over. (Most seed packets from reputable seed companies have good directions on them.) Water the soil. Sow the seeds thinly—otherwise the seedlings will choke each other as they try to grow—and then press the soil down lightly with a board.

The seeds can be sown where the plants are to grow—*Anthriscus Cerefolium*

(Chervil), for example, hates being moved—and then thinned out to the required distance apart when the seedlings are 2-3 inches high. Alternatively, sow them in seed compost in a seed box, and plant the seedlings out when they are large enough to handle.

If you have a greenhouse or frame you can sow many of the annuals a month early so as to be ready for planting outside when there is no longer any danger of frost.

In dry periods the seedlings need almost constant attention, and careful watering with a fine rose on the watering can. Hand weeding between the tiny plants is important, too.

Many of the annual herbs only take from two to three months to flower, and if planted out at the beginning of the summer, will be ready to harvest at the end of it. *Borago Officinalis* (Borage) and *Satureja Hortensis* (Summer Savory) ripen particularly quickly (and Borage will seed itself happily all over the garden).

If you feel growing from seed entails too much time and trouble, do not despair, many of these annual herbs, like the perennials, can be bought as plants.

Growing plants and cuttings

The perennial herbs, and the annuals too if you prefer, are bought as plants or cuttings and put directly into the bed during the summer. Dig a hole with a trowel and if it is dry, fill the hole with water. Put in the plant and firm the soil back down around it so that it is well anchored in case of rain or gale. For the first two weeks protect the young plants from sun and wind, and water them carefully every evening.

Growing by root division

Mentha sp. (Mints) once planted are easy to keep going as they spread so energetically—their runners creeping across the soil and putting down roots at regular intervals. In spring just pull up these runners, break them off, and plant them out alone.

Care of the herb garden

Weeding is even more important in a herb garden than in a flower garden. Each plant, clump, or row must stand alone. They need to be kept tidy with no messy weeds or grass growing near. And label any perennial plants, such as *Inula Helenium* (Elecampane), and *Symphytum Officinale* (Comfrey) which are going to die down in the winter— or you may forget where they are.

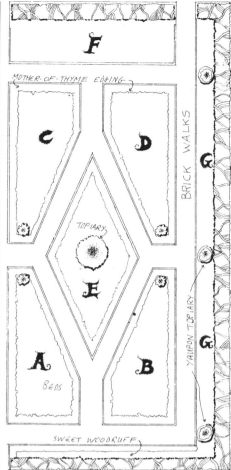

BED A
Sweet Majoram
Chamaedry's Germander
True Lavender
Rosemary
Yarrow
Garden Sage
Common Betony
Grass Pink

BED B
Chamaedry's Germander
True Lavender
Garden Sage
Common Betony
Yarrow
Common Rue
Common Hoarhound
Grass Pink

BED C
Oldman Wormwood
Woolly Betony
Chamaedry's Germander
Rosemary
Garden Sage
Sweet Majoram
Common Fennel
Yarrow
Tarragon
Lemon Verbena

BED D
Chamaedry's Germander
Oldman Wormwood
True Lavender
Common Rue
French Sorrel
Common Betony
Yarrow
Hyssop
Costmary

BED E
SPRING:
Mixed Crocus
Blue and White
    Hyacinth
Mixed Pansies
SUMMER:
Orange French
    Marigold

BED F
SPRING:
Yellow Crocus
Yellow Pansy
SUMMER:
African Marigold
    (Yellow)
French Marigold
    (Yellow)

BED G
Common Tansy
Candytuft

The John Blair Herb Garden (left)
in Williamsburg, USA, was designed
as recently as 1937, yet it has a simple
formality reminiscent of much older,
traditional gardens.

herbs for the kitchen

Preserving herbs

There is nothing like the taste of fresh herbs but, when they are not available fresh, many can be successfully used in cooking in a dried or frozen state.

The herbs which, perhaps, dry best of all are Thyme and Marjoram. (In Greece they dry the flowers of marjoram, not the leaves, these keep very well, are called *rigani* and are responsible for the distinctive flavour of Greek kebabs.) Chives, Chervil, Dill and Fennel leaves are the least worthwhile of dried herbs. But the seeds of Dill and Fennel, and Fennel stalks dried in the sun, can be used to flavour fish, chicken and pork.

When to pick

If you are going to use the **leaf** pick the herb for drying when the flowers are just in bud—the aromatic oils are then at their most pungent.

Harvest **flowers** just before they are fully open. If you are going to candy them then drop them into water for a minute or two to wash away earwigs.

Where the **seeds** of the herbs are used —Lovage, Dill, Fennel and Coriander —gather them when the heads turn brown. Test to see if they are ready by gently turning them upside down and shaking. If the seeds fall they are ready to pick.

Herbs, like any flowers or plants, are best picked in the early morning before the sun has reached them, but after dew has gone—most herbs are extremely difficult to handle when wet. Use a sharp knife, and put the cut herbs into a flat basket. Avoid crushing them as they will then lose their fragrance, and do not gather more herbs than you can deal with quickly. As little time as possible must elapse between picking and drying or the aroma is lost.

Harvesting Marjoram (top right), drying Garlic in the sun (bottom left), and in small bunches in the kitchen (top left) and the final result (bottom right).

How to Dry

All herbs should be dried in an airy, shady place where there is no danger of condensation.

Air drying. The easiest method, when possible, is to cut sprays, tie them into bunches, and hang them upside down to dry in an airy loft or spare room—or the garage if it is not damp and there are no petrol fumes. They should be dry within two or three weeks. They are ready when they are brittle to the touch.

Quick-drying. The faster the method of drying the more of the essential basic aroma is retained, so a quick-drying method is usually preferable. Spread the herbs on newspaper, cotton, muslin or nylon stretched over a cake tray or frame. Then put them in a warm, dry place. Look at the herbs after 12 hours. Like air dried herbs they are ready when brittle to the touch. Allow them to cool thoroughly, then store them.

Storing

Strip leaves from their stems, crumble them—but not too finely or they will quickly lose their flavour—and put them into clean, air-tight containers. Some herbs such as Sage, Thyme and Rosemary can be left on the stalk. (This makes them easier to put into casseroles and stews and remove when cooking is over.) Dried Bay leaves, too, can be kept on a long stalk. And they will all look very decorative stored in tall glass jars in a dark corner of the kitchen. Seeds and flower-heads can, of course, be put straight into a container.

If moisture starts to form on the inside of the container the herbs have not been dried correctly. Put them onto paper and allow a further drying time.

Deep freezing

Herbs, like so many other things, can be quickly and easily deep-frozen. Gather them in the morning. Wash them, and shake off any water. Then put them into plastic freezer bags in the deep-freeze.

How long to keep them

Dried herbs in general last a year at the most, and the more finely powdered they are the sooner they lose their taste. It is a good idea to date your containers, so that you know exactly how long you have had the herbs. Lemon Balm, Parsley, Summer Savory and Tarragon only last nine months to a year when dried. Basil, Lovage, Mint and Marjoram last a year or more. And Rosemary, Sage and Thyme can last longer still—but it is a good idea to replace them yearly if you can.

Herbs in the kitchen

Herbs can improve so many dishes that it really is worth using them whenever possible. But be careful, it is very easy to add herbs with too liberal a hand and swamp the flavour of the dish itself.

Fresh or dried?

It is, of course, better to use fresh herbs in cooking, but where this is impossible dried ones can be substituted. (See this page for which herbs do and do not dry successfully.)

Remember that the flavour in the leaves of herbs tends to become much more concentrated with drying (although not with freezing) so you need a much smaller amount when cooking. Usually a third to half the amount you would use fresh is sufficient.

If you are forced to rely on dried herbs a lot then keep fresh Parsley going for as long as possible. Sow rows again in late summer in a sheltered spot in the garden, or put some in a pot to grow indoors. This invaluable fresh-tasting herb is a great help in bringing out the flavour of all the dried herbs.

Bouquet Garni

The little bunches of herbs which make up a *Bouquet Garni* should be tied up with thread or string. Leave a long end coming out of the saucepan (tie it to the handle if you like, it does often fall in), so that you can remove the bouquet before serving. If you are using crumbled dried herbs, and do not want bits of leaf floating in your casserole or sauce, you can tie them into a small square of muslin or cheese-cloth.

The basic *Bouquet Garni*, which is as much a part of traditional French cooking as salt and pepper, consists of a little bunch of dried Thyme, a dried Bay leaf and fresh Parsley. (Or, of course, all fresh if this can be managed.) Some cooks like to add Rosemary to a *Bouquet Garni*. Experiment with this, but be wary—rosemary has a strong taste and can be overpowering. It is, however, good alone with roasts.

For fish dishes a bunch of fennel and bay is good. Use it with a little lemon rind, Lemon Balm or Lemon Verbena. For chicken a big sprig of Tarragon is excellent. Either add it to the basic *Bouquet Garni* or use it on its own.

Fines Herbes

Fines herbes, widely used in omelettes, are usually a mixture of Chervil, Chives, Parsley and Tarragon finely chopped and mixed together. As Chives and Chervil do not dry very well try to use fresh herbs if at all possible.

foods/ herbs to use with them

Soups
Basil, Bay, Chervil, Chives, Coriander, Dill, Lovage, Marjoram, Parsley, Sage, Savory, Sweet Cicely, Tarragon, Thyme.

Breads
Basil, Coriander, Dill, Fennel, Marjoram, Parsley, Savory, Thyme.

Fish
Basil, Bay, Dill, Lemon Balm, Lovage, Marjoram, Rosemary, Sage, Savory, Tarragon, Thyme.

Eggs
Basil, Bay, Chervil, Chives, Dill, Fennel, Garlic, Marjoram, Parsley, Rosemary, Savory, Tarragon, Thyme.

Shell-fish
Basil, Bay, Dill, Lemon Balm, Marjoram, Savory, Tarragon, Thyme.

Poultry
Basil, Bay, Dill, Lemon Balm, Lovage, Marjoram, Parsley, Rosemary, Sage, Savory, Tarragon, Thyme.

Lamb
Basil, Bay, Dill, Garlic, Marjoram, Mint, Rosemary, Sage, Savory, Tarragon, Thyme.

Beef
Basil, Bay, Chervil, Dill, Garlic, Marjoram, Parsley, Rosemary, Sage, Savory, Tarragon, Thyme.

Pork
Basil, Coriander, Dill, Fennel, Marjoram, Rosemary, Sage, Tarragon, Thyme.

Vegetables
Basil, Bay, Chervil, Coriander, Dandelion, Dill, Lovage, Marjoram, Mint, Parsley, Rosemary, Sage, Savory, Sweet Cicely, Salad Burnet, Tarragon, Thyme.

Cheeses
Basil, Chervil, Chives, Coriander, Dill, Mint, Nasturtium, Sage, Tarragon, Thyme.

Desserts
Bay, Coriander, Marigold, Thyme, Sweet Cicely, Lemon Verbena.

herbs/ uses in food and drink

Agrimony
Flowers, leaves and stem are used together for tea.

Angelica
The young scented leaves are used for tea, to flavour wines, and as an addition to sweet sauces. The candied stems are used to decorate cakes and desserts. (See recipe on page 35.)

Basil
The strongly-scented, almost flowery-smelling, sweet leaves are thought of mainly in connection with tomatoes, but are equally wonderful in all egg, cheese and vegetable dishes, can be used for teas and herb breads, can be chopped raw in salads and are used to flavour vinegar.
Basil is a vital ingredient in Pizza and many other Italian dishes. (The flavour increases when it is cooked, so greater quantities can be used raw.)

Bay
Bay leaves are an important part of a *Bouquet Garni*, and are indispensable for bacon and fish dishes and in marinades. They should always be added to stocks, stews and casseroles and are a valuable addition to patés and vegetable soups. Bay is also very good for sousing with herrings and mackerel. For most dishes, half to one Bay leaf is sufficient as the flavour is very strong, but two can be used with onion and cloves when boiling ham or tongue for a cold buffet.

Bergamot
The leaves are mainly used to make one of the best herb teas—refreshing, relaxing, and said to promote sleep. They can also be added to ordinary India or China tea, put into wine, and used to flavour hot milk.
The flowers and young leaves are decorative and can be used raw in salads.

Borage
The leaves have a cool, cucumbery taste and are used in wine cups with lemon, in iced tea, in summer fruit drinks, and, sometimes, with summer soups, vegetables, and salads, or to flavour vinegar.
The flowers can be used to decorate salads or cold fish dishes.

Camomile
The flowers are used for tea.

Catnip
The leaves are used for a medicinal tea.

Chervil
The leaves are good in all salads. (Use a lot as it has a very delicate, slightly aniseed taste.) They are also used in soups, egg, cheese and fish dishes, and mixed with Parsley and Chives in omelettes.

Chives
Chives are used whenever a mild onion taste is needed. Many cheese and egg dishes, soups, omelettes and stews can be sprinkled with finely cut or chopped Chives. They are delicious on new potatoes, carrots and turnips, and try them alone on bread and butter.

Coltsfoot
This whole plant is enormously rich in Vitamin C and both the leaves and the flowers can be used, fresh or dried, to make tea. The flowers are also used to make wine.

Coriander
The pungent aromatic seeds can be included in soups, ground over meat before grilling or frying, and used to flavour vinegars and vegetable dishes.
The young leaves can be used in soups in the same way as parsley, and raw in salads.

Dandelion
The young leaves are even more nutritious than spinach and are used in salads and as a pot herb in stocks and soups. They can also be cooked with other green vegetables such as spinach. And, of course, Dandelion makes excellent teas, beers and wines.

Dill
Both leaves and seeds are used to flavour vinegar. In summer the leaves can be added to salads, and bland or delicate vegetables. In winter the seeds are good in soups, stews, fish and rice dishes, and teas and bread.

Elder
The flowers are used dried to make a tea which tastes slightly of muscatel. They can also be dipped in batter and fried making excellent fritters. And try including a *Bouquet Garni* of three or four flower-heads in a bag when making gooseberry jam. (See page 19 for how to dry Elder flowers.) The berries can be added to blackberries for jams and tarts

and are, of course, the basis of a country wine very like port.

Fennel
Fennel stimulates the appetite and aids digestion. It tastes strongly of aniseed, and is used in a similar way to Dill. It is good with chicken, fish and egg dishes. The leaves can be used in herb vinegar, the seeds in breads and teas. Fresh leaves are used, but dried stems and seeds (see page 19).

Garlic
Garlic can be used to flavour salads, soups, casseroles, roast meats and vinegar. It is, of course, vital to taramasalata and Garlic bread.

Good King Henry, Mercury
The nutritious young leaves are used as a substitute for asparagus, and later in the summer the mature leaves as a substitute for spinach.

Horehound
A tea made by infusing the fresh or dried leaves is traditionally held to be good for colds.

Hyssop
The leaves have a slightly bitter, minty flavour and are not a great deal used in cooking. Used sparingly, they are, however, good in broths, stews, and fatty dishes, and can be made into a tea.

Lemon Balm
The leaves are mainly known for making the most wonderful tea, which is both calming and relaxing. They are also used in wine cups, as a substitute for lemon peel in soups and stews with lamb or fish, as a flavouring for custards and puddings, and chopped raw into salad dressings.

Lemon Verbena
The leaves are used to flavour custards, jams, drinks and in sauces for fish. They also make a good tea when mixed with a little Mint.

Lime
The flowers are used to make a relaxing tea—called *tilleul* in France, where it is extremely popular. The young leaves, picked in spring, also make a good tea.

Lovage
The seeds and both fresh and dried leaves are used. It is a strong herb tasting like a cross between celery and curry, so use it sparingly until you know it. It adds a 'meaty' flavour to foods, and is used in soups, stews and stocks.
The chopped leaves can be sprinkled on salads, and cheese and egg dishes.
Both leaves and seeds can be used to make a tea which tastes more like a broth.

Marigold
The petals are used in cakes and buns, on salads and as a substitute for saffron in colouring rice dishes.

Marjoram
The leaves are used with all meats, in casseroles and stews, with chicken, sausage, tomato, mushroom and egg dishes. They are also good with pulses and potatoes, in stuffings and bread, with salads, and as a flavouring to vinegars and wine cups.

Meadowsweet
The leaves and flowers are used for tea.

Mint
Mint leaves are used extensively in meat cookery, particularly in the well-known form of Mint sauce as an accompaniment to lamb. They are excellent chopped and sprinkled over new potatoes, salads and spring vegetables. They can be used in omelettes and in yogurt and cucumber salads, and are excellent made into a tea, used as an addition to wine cups or in Mint Juleps.

Mugwort
This highly aromatic herb is not greatly used in cooking, but the chopped leaves are good added to fatty or indigestible meat or goose dishes.

Nasturtium
The young leaves are rich in Vitamin C and give a peppery, sharp flavour to salads, sandwiches and cheese dishes, but use them with care and in moderation. The flowers are lovely in salads, and the young green seeds make a good substitute for capers.

Nettle
The young leaves are cooked as a vegetable and used for Nettle beer. Nettle tea is good, too.

Parsley
There is practically no dish which Parsley will not improve. It is a garnish, and tempting sprinkled over vegetables, salads and soups; an essential part of the *Bouquet Garni* used in stews and soups; excellent in poultry stuffings; good in sauces, and delicious raw in sandwiches. It also makes a good tea.

Plantain
The fresh leaves can be used for tea.

Purslane
The young leaves are used raw in salads, and can be eaten as a cooked vegetable.

Rocket
The young leaves are used in salads, or cooked with other green leafy vegetables.

Rosemary
Rosemary is strong and aromatic, so use it sparingly. Add it to meat, game, fish, egg, and poultry dishes. It can be used in tea, and is excellent on grills and barbeques, and, of course, in stuffings.

Sage
Sage is traditionally used with all rich and fatty meats as its strong taste counteracts greasiness. Add it to liver, fish, cheese and onions, sausages, and,

of course, stuffings. Sage is a strong herb so use it with caution. And remember the leaves make a good spring tonic tea.

Salad Burnet
The green cucumbery tasting leaves can be used all winter, and are good in soups, sauces and salads. Use them, too, in wine cups and drinks in the same way as Borage, and for a tea which is cleansing to the whole system.

Savory
This is traditionally the herb cooked with all bean dishes to increase the flavour and make them more digestible. It is good in stuffings and casseroles, can be chopped into salads, and is excellent with cucumber, lentils, pork and trout. The leaves can also be used in herb vinegar.

Sorrel
Sorrel leaves have a fresh, tangy, lemony taste and make delicious soup.

Sunflower
The buds of Sunflowers are sometimes used in salads, and the seeds are delicious roasted, salted and eaten like peanuts.

Sweet Cicely
The chopped leaves and stems of Sweet Cicely reduce the acidity in fruits such as gooseberries, currants and rhubarb, and can halve the quantity of sugar used to sweeten them—so they are good for anyone on a sugar-reduced diet.
It is also good in all salad dressings and soups and can be cooked with cabbage and root vegetables.

Tarragon
The leaves are used in sauces, (in France a famous sauce, Béarnaise, is based on Tarragon), and added to marinades, salads and stuffings. Tarragon is good with fish, eggs, shellfish, and poultry, and excellent sprinkled over new potatoes with butter and lemon. It also makes a good flavouring for wine vinegar.

Thyme
This is one of the three herbs that make up a basic *Bouquet Garni*, and is, of course, used in stuffings. It is good with cheeses, all meat dishes, and vegetables such as carrots and turnips, and it also makes a good tea. It has a strong flavour so use it with caution.

Vervain
The leaves are used in France to make a tea which is slightly bitter and good for the digestion.

Violet
The leaves are used for tea, and the flowers can be candied.

Woodruff
The leaves are used for tea and added to wine, apple and cider drinks.

Yarrow
The leaves are used for tea.

about the recipes

Herbs can be added to food and drink in so many different ways and using so many different combinations of herbs that it is difficult to include them all. However, on the following pages there are recipes for teas, breads, vinegars, drinks and foods—all of which are made with herbs. These have been divided into various categories, and unless otherwise stated the quantities given are for fresh herbs. Normally you only need half to a third the amount given if you are using dried herbs instead of fresh ones. Below are all the recipes for herb teas, together with the reputed medicinal uses of these teas. Recipes for herb breads have been gathered together, as have those for the wine cups or beers made with or using herbs. On page 26 there are recipes for making herb oils and vinegar. The food section has been split into two. On pages 30-31 there are hints on quick, easy ways of improving food by adding herbs, and some easy recipes for herb sauces and stuffings. And on pages 32-43 are recipes for soups, main courses, etc., which, for easy reference, have been listed under the herb which is used in them. So if, for example, you want to find a meat recipe which uses Basil you just look under Basil rather than having to look through a long list of main course recipes.

   All the recipes are reasonably easy to make, and do not include expensive ingredients. Each gives the number of servings and approximate preparation and cooking time required. And for a quick visual guide the recipes also have the following symbols:

★   This indicates that the dish does not need cooking.

⊠   This is a guide to the total cooking time—from initial preparation to serving. The time required for each dish will vary according to the skill of the individual cook.

⊠   Less than 1 hour

⊠ ⊠   Between 1 hour and 2½ hours

⊠ ⊠ ⊠   Over 2½ hours

teas for health and pleasure

These have been known and enjoyed for centuries both as refreshing drinks and as aids to the digestion. Many of them, too, are still used in country districts and by homeopathic pharmacists for medicinal purposes. The ailments they are reputed to help cure are given but cannot be vouched for.

If you use dried herbs for the tea allow 1 teaspoon for each cup and one for the pot. If you use fresh leaves, then you need 3 teaspoons per cup.

All the teas are made in the normal way. Just warm the pot, put in the herbs, pour in boiling water, and allow to steep for 5-10 minutes.

Some teas are made from the seeds of herbs. Pound the seeds in a mortar— dill, fennel, or lovage are generally used —then simmer them in boiling water for 5-10 minutes.

The most common herb teas, using the leaves and flowers of the plants, are listed below, together with any generally recognized medicinal properties they may have.

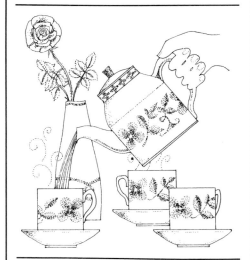

Agrimony.
Angelica. The young leaves can be made into a tea which is good for nervous headaches.
Basil. This can be served hot or cold, and is soothing and good for colds and gastric upsets.
Bergamot. This relaxing and sleep-inducing tea can be used alone or as an addition to China tea.
Borage. This is a refreshing tonic-tea, and can be served iced.

Camomile. A tea made from the dried flowers is popular in France.
Catnip. This makes a tonic tea, good for feverishness and nervous headaches.
Coltsfoot. The flowers can be used fresh or dried to make a tea which is used to treat catarrh and chest troubles.
Dandelion. The fresh or dried leaves make a tea which is allegedly good for all rheumatic conditions and digestive upsets.
Elder. A tea made from Elder flowers is soothing and supposedly good for cold and throat infections.
Horehound. This is good for coughs and colds.
Hyssop. This makes a cleansing tonic tea.
Lemon Balm. This makes another soothing, relaxing drink.
Lemon Verbena. Mixed with a few Mint leaves this makes a delicious tea.
Lime. The flowers are used to make a fragrant, soothing tea, particularly good to drink just before going to bed.
Lovage. This makes a cleansing and refreshing tea, more like a broth, and is usually seasoned with salt.
Meadowsweet. The flowers are used for a tea to alleviate diarrhoea, dysentery and colic.
Mint. This is a refreshing tea which is good for stomach aches.
Nettle. This makes a very good health giving and blood-purifying tea.
Parsley.
Plantain. The fresh green leaves are used to make tea.
Rosemary. This makes a tea which helps to cure headaches.
Sage. This tea is used as a tonic.
Salad Burnet.
Thyme. This tea is useful for coughs and sinus ailments.
Vervain. A slightly bitter tea, this is taken as a digestive or drunk last thing in the evening as a sedative.
Violet. The leaves are used to make a refreshing and stimulating tonic tea.
Woodruff.
Yarrow. This tea has a slightly bitter taste, but it is very good for colds and chest complaints.

Herb teas are relaxing and delicious (left), and many of them also have medicinal and digestive properties.

herb breads

Making your own bread is one of the greatest pleasures in cooking, and there are subtle and delicious bread recipes which use both seeds and dried herbs. Experiment with different flavours, Dill and Fennel go well with bread, as do dried Marjoram, Basil and Thyme. It is easy to overdo the flavouring, so start by using only a little, you can add more next time if you like.

Garlic Bread

Garlic bread is, of course, well known and very simple to prepare. Crush 2 or 3 cloves of Garlic, mix with softened butter and spread down the middle of a French loaf. Wrap the bread in foil and crisp it in the oven. Always serve garlic bread hot.

Basic Herb Bread

Any dried herb can be introduced to this delicately-flavoured bread which is easy to make.
Preparation and cooking time:
3 hours 45 minutes
TWO 1 POUND LOAVES

¾ tablespoon dried yeast or
    ¾ oz. fresh yeast
½ pint [1¼ cups] water, lukewarm
1 lb. bread flour
1 tablespoon sugar
2 teaspoons salt
¾ teaspoon dried marjoram, or
    basil, or thyme

Dissolve the yeast in half of the lukewarm water and leave for 15 to 20 minutes in a warm place. Stir together in a bowl the other ingredients, add the foamy yeast and water mixture and the remaining water and mix well until the dough comes away from the side of the bowl with a spatula. Add enough of the remaining water to make a sticky dough. Mix with a spatula or in a machine with a dough-hook. Turn out onto a heavily-floured board and knead for 5 to 10 minutes. Set aside to rise for 1 to 1½ hours or until doubled in bulk.

Heat the oven to 475 °F (Gas Mark 9, 240 °C).
When the dough has risen punch it down and divide the mixture into 1 or 2 loaves. Knead firmly for 3 or 4 minutes then put straight into an oiled 2-pound bread tin or 2 1-pound tins or put onto a baking sheet. Leave to rise again for about 1 hour. Bake in the oven for 10 minutes, then lower the oven temperature to 425 °F (Gas Mark 7, 220 °C) and bake for a further 30 minutes or until the bread is brown on top and gives a hollow sound when knocked.

Elsinore Bread

Preparation and cooking time: 3½ hours
ONE 1 POUND LOAF

4 oz. [½ cup] cottage cheese, warm
¼ pint [⅝ cup] water, lukewarm
½ tablespoon dried yeast or
    ½ oz. fresh yeast
2 tablespoons sugar
½ oz. [1 tablespoon] butter, melted
1 tablespoon dill seed
1 teaspoon salt
12 oz. [3 cups] flour
1 egg
¼ teaspoon baking powder

Dissolve the yeast in 4 tablespoons of the warm water, and leave to stand for 15 to 20 minutes.
Mash the melted butter and egg into the warm cottage cheese. Add the frothy yeast mixture, stir well, then add the rest of the water and stir again. Add the dry ingredients and mix to make a good stiff dough. Turn onto a floured board and knead for 3 to 4 minutes. Place in a greased bowl and leave to rise for 1 to 1½ hours until it doubles in bulk.
Heat the oven to 475 °F (Gas Mark 9 240 °C).
Take the ball of dough and knead gently on a floury board then put into a buttered or oiled 1-pound bread tin or 2 small bread tins and leave to rise for 1 hour.
Bake in the oven for 10 minutes then lower the oven temperature to moderate 425 °F (Gas Mark 7, 220 °C), and bake for a further 25 minutes or until brown.

Herby Soda Bread

Preparation and cooking time: 1 hour
ONE ¾ POUND LOAF

8 oz. [2 cups] bread flour and 1 teaspoon baking powder, or 8 oz. [2 cups] self-raising flour
4 oz. [¾ cup] raisins or sultanas
2 tablespoons sugar
¼ teaspoon marjoram
¼ teaspoon basil
pinch of dried thyme
1 teaspoon salt
1 egg, beaten
5 tablespoons milk
½ oz. [1 tablespoon] butter, melted

Heat oven to 400 °F (Gas Mark 6, 200 °C).
Put the dry ingredients into a bowl and mix thoroughly. In another bowl beat together the egg, butter and milk. Add to the flour, herb and fruit mixture. Put onto a floured board and knead lightly. Put into a buttered cake tin and bake in the oven for 45 minutes.
Eat hot if possible.

Hungarian Fennel Bread

Here the bread mixture is divided up to give you little rolls.
Preparation and cooking time:
3-3½ hours
12 ROLLS

1½ lb. [6 cups] flour
2 teaspoons sugar
½ teaspoon salt
1 tablespoon fennel seeds
1 tablespoon dried yeast or
    1 oz. fresh yeast
4 oz. [½ cup] butter, melted
½ pint [1¼ cups] water, lukewarm

Dissolve the yeast in half of the lukewarm water and leave to stand for 15 to 20 minutes.
Mix together in a bowl the flour and the fennel seeds with the sugar and salt. Add the yeast mixture to this, then add the rest of the hot water and mix well. Pour in the melted butter. Knead on a lightly floured board. Cover and allow to stand in a warm place for 1 to 1½ hours until doubled in bulk.
Heat oven to 475 °F (Gas Mark 9, 240 °C).
Knead, and then form the dough into 12 balls on the floured board. Put onto a greased baking sheet, cover and leave to rise for another hour. Paint if desired with a little egg yolk and milk. Bake in the oven for 10 minutes, then lower the oven temperature to 425 °F (Gas Mark 7, 220 °C) and bake for a further 25 minutes.

herb vinegars

These vinegars have a marvellous flavour and will improve any salad or marinade—particularly in winter when the fresh herbs are unobtainable.

Excellent vinegars can be made using the leaves of one of the following:- Lemon Balm, Basil, Borage, Salad Burnet, Dill, Fennel, Marjoram, Summer Savory, Mint, Tarragon—which is, perhaps the favourite—or Thyme.

You can also make a mixed herb vinegar. One good one is made up of Summer Savory, Marjoram, Chives and Tarragon, another from Basil, Rosemary, Mint, Tarragon and Bay.

Vinegars using leaves

Use only fresh leaves to make a herb vinegar. Gather the leaves as for preserving herbs (see pages 18-19) and, in the case of the flowering herbs, just before the plants are in full bloom. You will need about the equivalent of two cups of leaves to a quart of vinegar.

Wash and dry the leaves and pack them loosely into a wide-mouthed glass jar. Pour in good vinegar; you can use either white or red wine vinegar, cider vinegar or malt vinegar.

It is generally held that white wine vinegar is best for Tarragon, Basil and Salad Burnet; cider vinegar for Mint, and red wine vinegar for Garlic.

Cover the jar tightly and put it where you will remember to shake it, or stir the contents with a wooden spoon, every other day.

After 10 days taste it. If it is not quite herby enough take out the herb leaves, strain, and start all over again.

When the vinegar is as strong as you want it, strain it into bottles through a funnel, and add a sprig of the herb to decorate the bottle.

Vinegars using seeds

You can also make vinegars from the aromatic seeds like Coriander and Dill. To make a seed vinegar you bruise the seeds in a pestle and mortar, using about two tablespoons of seeds to a quart of vinegar. Put them in a jar and pour on warmed vinegar. Cover the jar tightly and put it in a warm place for two weeks, shaking it from time to time. Strain the vinegar—using filter paper or a muslin bag—through a funnel into the bottles and cork tightly.

Garlic vinegar

Finally, it is worth bearing in mind that Garlic, too, can be used to flavour vinegar. Put Garlic cloves into the vinegar, leave them for 24 hours, and then remove them.

herb oils

These are really extremely simple to make and they look and smell as delicious as they taste.

Experiment with different herbs, using the leaf part only. Particularly lovely herb oils can be made using basil, fennel, rosemary, tarragon, thyme and, of course, for beauty preparations, lavender. If possible make your herb oils in summer as strong sunlight is needed for the aromatic oils of the herbs to mingle with the oil itself.

Crush the herbs in a pestle and mortar. Alternatively, put them through a blender. Then put 2 tablespoons of the crushed herbs into a half pint [10 fl.oz.] bottle. Add sunflower, corn or olive oil, filling the bottle only three-quarters full. Add one tablespoon of wine vinegar and cork the bottle tightly.

Put the bottle somewhere where it receives hot sunlight and leave it there for two or three weeks, shaking the bottle a couple of times a day. At the end of this time strain off the oil, and press any remaining oil out of the crushed herbs. Repeat the process—using freshly-cut herbs—until the oil is strong enough. You should be able to really smell the herb when you put a little of the oil onto the back of your hand.

If there is not enough sunshine to bring the flavour out of the herbs then you can put the bottles—tightly corked of course—into a double boiler and 'cook' them at just below boiling point for a few hours each day. The oil should be strong enough after seven or eight days of this treatment.

Finally, if you wish, you can for decorative purposes add a sprig of the dried herb to the bottle of oil.

herb drinks

There are many well-known wines and beers made from herbs—some of them more potent than the wines made from grapes, so beware. But you can, of course, add herbs to wine you have bought. Herb wines and wine cups have been popular for a very long time, and the famous Mrs. Beeton was very enthusiastic about them.

For a change try a leaf or two of Mint, or Salad Burnet or Lemon Balm added to white wine or cider.

Experiment with Borage. It is often put into winecups because it has an exhilarating effect. And the addition of just a leaf and a flower to a glass of chilled white wine with a little soda makes a marvellous drink for a hot summer day.

Champagne Cup

Preparation time: *10 minutes*
MAKES 10 GLASSES

1 large bottle of sparkling white wine
2 bottles soda water, or to taste
2 tablespoons sugar
1 small glass brandy
1 sprig of green borage
1 lb. crushed ice

Put all the ingredients into a large bowl or jug, stir well and serve.

Coltsfoot Wine

MAKES 1 GALLON OF WINE

1 gallon freshly-picked Coltsfoot flowers
3½ lb. sugar
2 oranges
2 lemons
1 teaspoon grape tannin
1 gallon water
¾ oz. fresh yeast *or*
1 level teaspoon dried brewers' yeast

Dissolve the sugar in the water and simmer for 5 minutes, then remove from heat and cool. Add a little of the liquid to the yeast and leave to activate. Peel the oranges and lemons thinly and squeeze them. Put the rinds and juice into a jar or well-covered clean plastic

Thyme vinegar or Tarragon olive oil (inset) will improve many dishes.

bucket with the tannin and the flowers. Pour in the sugar and water syrup and stir. Add the yeast mixture and leave to ferment in a warm place, well covered with a cloth. Stir daily. When the most active fermentation subsides strain into a glass fermenting jar, cork with an air lock, and leave to stand in a cool place. When fermentation stops siphon off and bottle.

Dandelion Wine

MAKES 1 GALLON OF WINE

2 quarts dandelion flowers
4 oranges
¾ oz. fresh yeast *or*
1 level teaspoon dried
    brewers' yeast
3 lbs. sugar
1 gallon water

Pick the flowers on a sunny day when they are dry and fully open and measure them into a quart jug. Boil the water, then pour it over the flowers and leave them to steep for two days, but no longer or the flavour will be impaired. *Peel* and juice the oranges. Boil up the flower and water mixture with the orange peel, then strain it onto the sugar. Stir until the sugar is dissolved. When the liquid is cool add the orange juice, yeast and nutrient.
Put the liquid into a glass fermenting jar and fit an air-lock. When fermentation has stopped and the wine is clear siphon into bottles and cork.
This wine can be drunk after six months but it is better if kept longer.

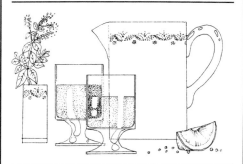

Claret Cup

Preparation time: *45 minutes*
MAKES 9 GLASSES

1 bottle claret
1 tablespoon sugar
2 tablespoons water, hot
1 zest of lemon
1 glass sherry
½ teaspoon grated nutmeg

7 or 8 leaves lemon verbena
1 bottle soda water or to taste
2 or 3 sprigs borage

Dissolve the sugar in a jug with the water. Add all the other ingredients except the borage and leave to stand for 30 minutes, then strain into a jug. *Ice* before serving and decorate the jug with a few sprigs of borage.

Hypocras

Preparation time: *4¼ hours*
MAKES 18 GLASSES

2 litres white wine
1 lb. brown sugar
1 teaspoon cinnamon
4 oz. [¾ cup] marjoram leaves
2 peppercorns
3 slices lemon

Mix all the ingredients together in a jug. Allow to stand for 4 hours. Strain, chill and serve.

Mint Julep

Preparation time: *5 minutes*
MAKES 1 GLASS

1 fl.oz. whiskey, Scotch or Irish, or
    Bourbon
crushed ice
4 mint leaves
1 teaspoon sugar

Put the ice in the glass. Add sugar (this can be made into a syrup with water), whiskey and mint. Stir and put in more ice and whiskey. Let it stand till the glass frosts.

Nettle Beer

MAKES 1 GALLON OF BEER

2 lbs. young nettle tops
1 lb. brown sugar
1 lemon
1 gallon water
½ oz. [1 tablespoon] root ginger
1 oz. [4 tablespoons] cream of tartar
¾ oz. fresh yeast *or*
1 level teaspoon dried brewers' yeast

Cut off the nettle roots; rinse the tops, drain, and boil in the water for 15 minutes together with the root ginger. Meanwhile rind and juice the lemon. Strain the nettle liquid into a bowl containing the lemon peel and juice,

sugar and cream of tartar. Stir well, leave to cool, add the yeast.
Keep covered with a cloth in a warm place for 3 days. Strain, bottle and cork. Keep a week or two before drinking.

Woodruff Cup

Woodruff makes the best early summer or May Drink and is a traditional drink in Germany—the 'Maitrunk'. *The* woodruff must be dry to make sure that the full aroma and flavour are present.
Preparation time: *1¼ hours*
MAKES 15 GLASSES

2 bottles dry white wine
3 or 4 sprigs woodruff
zest and juice of 1 lemon
½ lb. soft fruit (i.e. strawberries)
sugar to taste
2 bottles soda water, or to taste
mint or borage leaves

Put the woodruff and ½ bottle of the wine into a bowl, and leave to stand for ½-1 hour.
Filter or strain, discarding the woodruff and then add the rest of the wine, the lemon juice and rind, fruit, sugar and soda water. Decorate with mint or borage leaves and serve.

Strawberry Cup

For a really special drink you could substitute champagne for the soda water in this wine cup.
Preparation time: *3¼ hours*
MAKES 15 GLASSES

2 bottles white wine
2 sprigs sage, mint, lemon balm
    or marjoram, crushed
2 bottles soda water, or to taste
sugar
1 lb. strawberries

Put the herbs in a pot and pour in the wine. Cover and leave to stand for 3 hours in a cool place.
Lightly sugar the strawberries. Put them into the liquid and add the soda water before serving. Make sure that everybody gets some strawberries in the glass.

With decorative blue Borage flowers floating on top of it Claret cup with Borage (right) looks and tastes wonderful on a hot summer's day.

flavours, sauces and stuffings

Here are some quick and easy ways to transform the flavour and appearance of various foods by the addition of herbs—either by including them with the food or by making sauces or stuffings. None of these ideas call for much extra time to be spent in the kitchen, and the little extra effort that goes into them is more than compensated for by added flavour.

Fish

Fish pie with Chives
This is a simple, and unusual way of cooking fish.
Poach fillets of haddock or cod, and flake. Make ½ pint of white sauce and mix with the fish. Season to taste and add Nutmeg if you wish. Sprinkle chopped fresh Chives on top and brown in a moderate oven.

Grilled fish with Fennel
Fennel mixes well with red mullet, bass, and other fish, and is a simple delicious addition to grilled fish.
Clean and salt the fish and put some chopped Fennel and Sage inside them. Slit the sides twice, and coat with oil. Put a bed of Fennel leaves and stems in a pan and put the fish on top. Cook, turning and brushing with oil. Serve garnished with lemon.

Meat

Chops and Coriander
The flavour of coriander blends well with both pork and veal chops.
Dip the chops in a mixture of flour, egg and breadcrumbs to which you have added crushed Garlic, and Coriander seed crushed or milled in a pepper mill. Then cook in the normal way.

Roast lamb and pork with Coriander
Lamb and pork are delicious with Coriander. Make small cuts in the skin and rub crushed Garlic and Coriander into them before roasting in the usual way.

Roast lamb with Garlic
A roast leg or shoulder of lamb is immensely improved by making deep cuts in the meat, inserting 2 or 3 cloves of Garlic, and then roasting in the usual way.

Steak with Basil butter
Fry fillet steaks in the usual way in oil or butter, and before serving put some Basil butter on each steak.
To make the Basil butter, chop basil leaves, and pound them in a mortar with a clove of Garlic and some salt. Then mix in an ounce [*2 tablespoons*] of butter.

Vegetables

Baked potatoes with mint
Bake potatoes in the usual way, then split them open and spoon over them a mixture of cream cheese, crushed Garlic and a good helping of chopped fresh Mint.

Potato cakes
Cook 4 or 5 potatoes and mash and beat with butter when hot. Add 1 tablespoon chopped fresh Chives. Allow to cool then add 1 beaten egg. Shape into flat cakes and fry in butter.

Green salad with Garlic
Garlic has a strong flavour and just rubbing the salad bowl with a sliced clove of Garlic is enough to give a salad a Garlic taste.

Spring vegetables with Mint
Mint is delicious with young potatoes, carrots, turnips, peas and green beans. Cook the vegetables in boiling water for 10 to 15 minutes until they are cooked but not soft. Strain, season, then return to the heat for a moment and stir in a generous knob of butter and 2 tablespoons of chopped fresh Mint.

Tomato Salad with Basil
Slice the tomatoes and put them in a bowl with a little finely chopped onion and a crushed clove of Garlic. Add oil (3 tablespoons for an average bowl) and a squeeze of lemon juice. Stir and sprinkle with chopped Basil to taste.

Thyme marrows
Thinly slice a vegetable marrow (or you can substitute courgettes [*zucchini*]). Put in a saucepan with 2 tablespoons of butter, salt and pepper, and 1 teaspoon chopped fresh Thyme. Cook gently, covered, for 12 minutes or until they are tender.

Cheeses

Cheese with Borage
The light cucumbery taste of Borage goes well with cheese.
Chop Borage leaves finely and mix them in a bowl of cream cheese, cottage cheese or Ayrshire cheese.

Chive cheese
Cream cheese, cottage cheese or Ayrshire cheese is given a delicious unusual taste if you season it with salt, pepper and lemon juice, add a handful of chopped fresh Chives and mix well.

Desserts

Fruit crumble with Coriander
Make an ordinary crumble—½ lb. [*2 cups*] flour, ¼ lb. [*⅓ cup*] butter, ¼ lb. [*⅓ cup*] sugar—to cover fruit like apple or strawberry, and sprinkle with a teaspoon of crushed Coriander seed. This makes a good alternative to ginger, which is given in some recipes.

Stewed fruit with Sweet Cicely
It is always a matter of taste how much sugar you use with fruit. Generally speaking it is 3-4 oz. [⅓-½ *cup*] sugar to 5-10 fl.oz. water to 1 lb. fruit.
Put a handful of stems and leaves of Sweet Cicely into the water and sugar before adding the fruit, so that the quantity of sugar can be reduced from by half or more. This herb is particularly good with the sharper fruits like rhubarb and gooseberries which usually need more sugar.

Béarnaise Sauce

This sauce is excellent served with steak.
Preparation and cooking time:
30 minutes
MAKES 7 FLUID OUNCES OF SAUCE

2 tablespoons white wine or wine
   vinegar
1 teaspoon finely-chopped onion or
   shallot
1 bay leaf
1 teaspoon chopped fresh tarragon
1 teaspoon chopped fresh chervil
2 egg yolks
1½ oz. [3 tablespoons] butter
5 fl.oz. stock
salt and pepper

Put the wine in a small pan with the onion, Bay leaf, Tarragon and Chervil and boil until reduced by about half. Strain. Mix the egg yolks with 1 tablespoon of the stock and put in the top of a double boiler or in a bowl over boiling water. Stir.
Add butter. Stir until thick and gradually add the rest of the stock. Add the wine mixture. Season to taste and if you like, add more Tarragon and Chervil before serving.

Fennel Sauce

Fennel is a flavour that goes well with fish, and this butter sauce will brighten up any fish dish.
Preparation and cooking time:
5 minutes
MAKES 4 FLUID OUNCES OF SAUCE

4 oz. [½ cup] butter
2 tablespoons chopped fresh
    fennel
salt

Melt the butter, add the Fennel, and season with salt.

Lemon Verbena Sauce

This sauce is delicious used with fish or chicken.
Preparation and cooking time:
25 minutes
MAKES 5 FLUID OUNCES OF SAUCE

3-4 fresh lemon verbena leaves
5 fl.oz. milk
½ tablespoon butter
½ tablespoon flour

Simmer the Lemon Verbena leaves in the milk for 10-15 minutes. Remove the leaves. Melt the butter and cook the flour in it, then gradually add the fragrant milk to make a white sauce. Chopped Lemon Balm leaves could be stirred in before serving.

Fresh Mint Sauce

This is, of course, the traditional accompaniment to roast lamb. It is usually made with white wine vinegar or malt vinegar, but for a change try this recipe which substitutes lemon juice. And for the nearest thing to fresh Mint sauce in the winter, simply chop the Mint in the summer, and fill

a screw-topped jar with alternate layers of mint and golden syrup [light corn syrup]. When the time comes to use it, just add vinegar or lemon juice.
Preparation time:
5 minutes, plus 1 hour to infuse
MAKES 2 FLUID OUNCES OF SAUCE

2 tablespoons chopped fresh mint
½ tablespoon sugar
1 tablespoon water, warm
juice of 2 lemons

Mix all the ingredients together and allow to stand for at least an hour.

Parsley Sauce

This sauce is excellent served with fish or beans.
Preparation and cooking time:
10 minutes
MAKES 10 FLUID OUNCES OF SAUCE

1 tablespoon butter
1 tablespoon flour
10 fl.oz. milk
3 tablespoons chopped fresh parsley

Make a roux with the butter and flour. Slowly add the milk, and cook gently for 5 minutes.
Just before serving, add the Parsley.

Pesto

This Genoese sauce is marvellous with all pasta dishes and as a flavouring for soups.
Preparation time: *20 minutes*
MAKES 8 FLUID OUNCES OF SAUCE

1 bunch fresh basil
2 cloves garlic
salt
8 fl.oz. olive oil
2 tablespoons grated Parmesan
    cheese

Pound the Basil leaves in a mortar with the Garlic and a little salt. When it is well mixed add the oil, a little at a time, and the cheese. Stir well until it is the consistency of thick cream.

Mugwort Stuffing

This stuffing is used with fatty or greasy meats—goose, pork, etc.—instead of, or, as in this recipe, as well as, sage.

Preparation and cooking time:
20 minutes
MAKES 10 OUNCES OF STUFFING

2 large onions, finely chopped
1 oz. [2 tablespoons] butter
1 tablespoon chopped fresh
    mugwort
4 oz. [1 cup] white breadcrumbs
1 tablespoon chopped sage
salt and pepper

Put the chopped onions in a pan with cold water and boil for 10 minutes until tender. Drain and add them to the other ingredients and mix well.

Sage and Onion Stuffing

This stuffing can be used with most meats, but is particularly good with pork or turkey.
Preparation and cooking time:
20 minutes
MAKES 12 OUNCES OF STUFFING

1 lb. onions, finely chopped
salt and pepper
4 oz. [1 cup] breadcrumbs
1-2 teaspoons finely-chopped fresh
    sage
1 oz. [2 tablespoons] butter

Put the onions and salt in a pan and simmer in water for 10 minutes. Strain, reserving the cooking water.
Mix the onion with the other ingredients and add enough of the cooking water to make a smooth paste.

Thyme Stuffing

This stuffing is, of course, the one traditionally used with poultry dishes.
Preparation and cooking time:
15 minutes
MAKES 6 OUNCES OF STUFFING

3 oz. [¾ cup] breadcrumbs
2 oz. [¼ cup] butter
1 tablespoon chopped onion
grated rind and juice of 1 lemon
salt and pepper
1 tablespoon chopped fresh thyme
½ tablespoon chopped fresh parsley
½ tablespoon chopped marjoram
1 egg, beaten

Melt the butter in a pan and cook the onion gently until golden. Put into a bowl with all the other ingredients and bind with the egg.

the recipes

Some of the dishes you can make using herbs: Apple Cider Mackerel with Bouquet Garni, see recipe on page 36 (above); Basil Pesto, see recipe on page 31 (left); Sausage and Apple Flan with Parsley, see recipe on page 41 (right) and (inset) a summer salad decorated with Marigold petals.

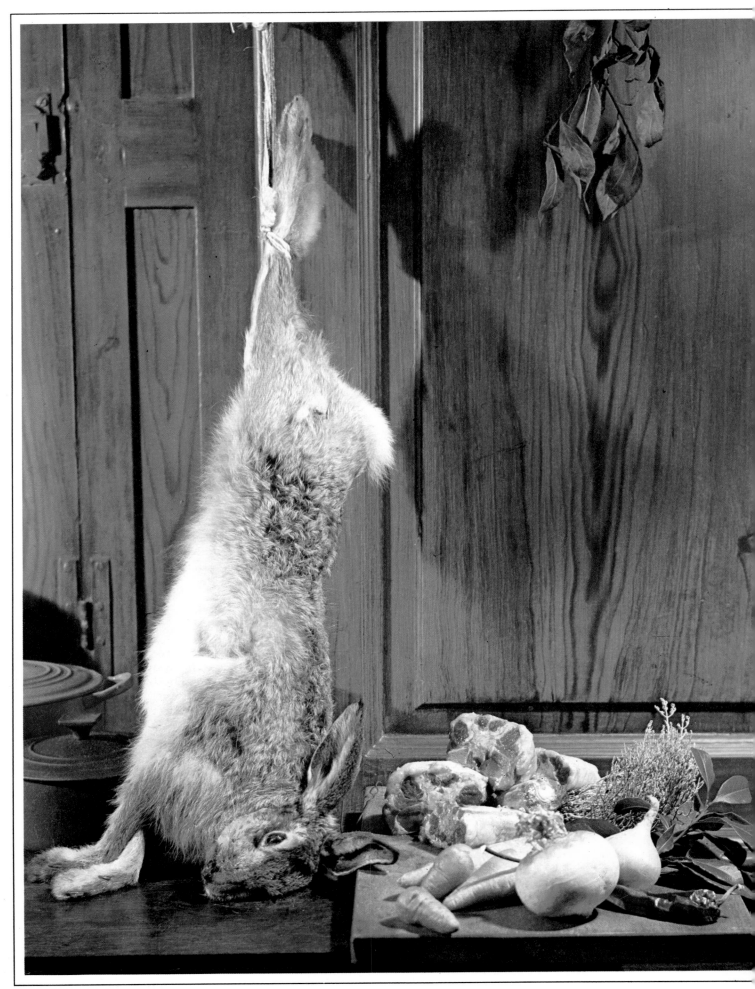

Angelica
Crystallized Angelica

This is a time-consuming task but, for those who like crystallized angelica, well worth it.
Cut young angelica stems in Spring and chop them into pieces 2-3 inches long. Put them in a bowl and cover them with boiling brine ($\frac{1}{4}$ lb. salt to 2 quarts water). Soak for 10 minutes then rinse in cold water. Boil the angelica in plain water for 5-10 minutes or until tender. Drain and scrape off the outer skin.
Allowing the same weight of white sugar to that of the angelica stems, dissolve the sugar in 10 fl.oz. water, add the angelica and bring to the boil again, then remove the stems and put them in another pan. Add $\frac{1}{2}$ lb. [1 cup] sugar to the liquid in the first pan, bring to the boil and then pour the liquid over the stems in the second pan.
Repeat this process every day for 4 days then leave the stems to soak in the syrup for 2 weeks. Take out, drain, and store between layers of waxed or greaseproof paper in a tin or box.

Basil
Baked Tomatoes

Preparation and cooking time:
30 minutes
SERVES 2-4

1 lb. tomatoes, sliced
1 clove garlic, crushed
2 onions, peeled and chopped
1 tablespoon chopped fresh basil
salt and pepper
1 oz. [$\frac{1}{3}$ cup] breadcrumbs
1 oz. [2 tablespoons] butter

Heat oven to 350°F (Gas Mark 4, 180°C).
Place the tomato slices on a buttered dish, with the garlic.
Mix the onions with the basil and sprinkle over the tomatoes. Season to taste. Sprinkle with breadcrumbs and dot with butter. Bake in the oven for 20 minutes.

Pizza with Basil

Preparation and cooking time:
45 minutes
SERVES 6-8

$\frac{3}{4}$ lb. pizza dough *or*
  plain short pastry
1 clove garlic, crushed
1 teaspoon chopped fresh basil
1 tablespoon oil
2 oz. [$\frac{1}{2}$ cup] cheese, grated
1 lb. tomatoes, sliced
1 tablespoon parsley, chopped
1 oz. [2 tablespoons] butter

Heat oven to 400°F (Gas Mark 6, 200°C).
Line two 8-inch tins with the dough or pastry, or put it onto a baking sheet. Mix together the garlic, basil and oil with 2 tablespoons of the grated cheese and spread this mixture on the dough. Put the tomatoes on top, cover with chopped parsley and the rest of the grated cheese, and dot with butter. Bake in the oven for 15 to 20 minutes.

Soupe au Pistou

A Mediterranean vegetable soup.
Preparation and cooking time: *1 hour*
SERVES 6-8

1 onion
2 leeks
1 oz. [2 tablespoons] butter
2 tomatoes, peeled and sliced
1$\frac{1}{2}$ pints [3$\frac{3}{4}$ cups] stock or water
4 potatoes, peeled and quartered
$\frac{1}{2}$ lb. green beans, diced
salt and pepper

For the pistou:
4 leaves fresh basil
2 cloves garlic
1 tablespoon olive oil
1 tablespoon grated Parmesan
  cheese

Chop the onion and leeks and sauté them in the butter until soft. Add the tomatoes, stock or water, potatoes and green beans. Season to taste. Cover and simmer for 40 minutes.
Meanwhile make the Pistou. Crush the basil and the garlic with olive oil in a mortar. Then add the cheese.
Add the Pistou to the soup just before serving.

Bay
Braised Beef

This dish is delicious served with noodles.
Preparation and cooking time:
3$\frac{1}{2}$ hours, plus 48 hours to marinate

SERVES 6-8

3 lbs. topside [topround] of beef
butter or oil
5 fl.oz. stock
1 oz. [4 tablespoons] flour
10 fl.oz. cream
salt
For the marinade:
2 wine glasses red wine
1 tablespoon wine vinegar
1 carrot, sliced
1 onion, sliced
4 cloves
1 bay leaf
1 sprig fresh thyme
1 teaspoon dry mustard
6 peppercorns
salt

Put all the marinade ingredients into a bowl or pan. Marinate the meat in this mixture for 48 hours, turning it several times.
Heat oven to 300°F (Gas Mark 2, 150°C).
Drain the meat and brown on all sides in the butter or oil in a flameproof casserole. Pour the marinade and stock over it and cook, covered, in the oven for 3 hours. Strain the sauce and thicken it with the flour, bring to the boil then simmer for 3 minutes. Then stir in the cream.
Slice the meat and pour the sauce over it.

Rabbit or Hare Stew

Preparation and cooking time: *2 hours*
SERVES 4-6

1 rabbit or hare, cut into pieces
1 oz. [4 tablespoons] seasoned flour
2 oz. [$\frac{1}{4}$ cup] butter
1 lb. tomatoes, peeled
1 lb. carrots, peeled and sliced
1 onion, chopped *or* a handful of
  fresh chives
1 lb. potatoes, peeled and sliced
1 wineglass red wine
1 bay leaf
$\frac{1}{2}$ teaspoon chopped fresh thyme
1 lb. turnips, peeled and sliced

Heat oven to 350°F (Gas Mark 4, 180°C).
Roll the rabbit pieces in the seasoned flour, and fry them in the butter until brown. Put into an ovenproof dish and add all the other ingredients. Cover and cook in a moderate oven for 1$\frac{1}{2}$ hours.

Ingredients for Hare Stew (left).

Bouquet Garni
Apple Cider Mackerel

This is an unusual fish dish.
Preparation and cooking time:
45 minutes
SERVES 4

2 mackerel
cider
1 tablespoon vinegar
1 bay leaf
juice of $\frac{1}{2}$ lemon
bouquet garni
salt and pepper

For the Sauce:
2 oz. [$\frac{1}{4}$ cup] **butter**
3 oz. [$\frac{3}{8}$ cup] **sugar**
2 lb. **cooking apples**
cider
To garnish: **lemon slices**

Heat oven to 375°F (Gas Mark 5, 190°C).
Clean and prepare the mackerel and place in an ovenproof dish. Add cider and vinegar to come half-way up the fish. Add the bay leaf, lemon juice and bouquet garni. Season to taste with salt and freshly ground black pepper.
Cook in the oven for 15 minutes.
To make the sauce melt the butter in a heavy saucepan; add sugar and cook until golden. Peel, core and quarter apples and add to butter-sugar mixture with cider. Cover and simmer till soft. Strain through a fine sieve.
Garnish the fish with lemon slices and serve the sauce separately.

Garbure

This recipe, using the traditional bouquet garni of thyme, bay and parsley makes a good stout soup for a cold day.
Preparation and cooking time: *1$\frac{1}{2}$ hours*
SERVES 6-8

1 large cabbage
3 large potatoes
3 large carrots
$\frac{1}{2}$ lb. **haricot [dried white] beans,** cooked
1 ham bone *or*
    $\frac{1}{4}$ lb. fatty bacon
1 bouquet garni
2 pints [5 cups] cold water
salt and pepper
1 tablespoon goose fat if available

Shred the cabbage, slice the potatoes and carrots, and put them all into a large soup pan with the haricot beans, the ham bone or bacon and the bouquet garni. Pour on the cold water and bring to the boil. Simmer for about 1 hour.
Remove the bouquet garni and season to taste. Remove the meat, cut the rind off the bacon or pick any meat off the ham bone. Chop the meat and return to the soup. Mash the vegetables lightly with a wooden spoon, and before serving add the goose fat if available.

Gigot à la Bretonne

Preparation and cooking time:
2$\frac{1}{4}$ hours, plus 8 hours soaking time for the haricot beans
SERVES 3-5

5 oz. [1 cup] **haricot [dried white] beans**
1 large onion
salt and pepper
1 bouquet garni
2-3 lb. **leg of lamb or mutton**
1 clove garlic, sliced
2 oz. [$\frac{1}{4}$ cup] **butter**
1 shallot, chopped
1 large tomato, peeled and quartered

Soak the haricot beans for 8 hours or overnight. Put the beans and the whole onion in a large saucepan with salt, pepper and the bouquet garni.
Cover with water and bring slowly to the boil, then simmer for 1 hour or until the beans are soft. Skim frequently. Strain, reserve the beans and onion and keep them warm.
Heat oven to 375°F (Gas Mark 5, 190°C).
Slit the surface of the meat and press the garlic slices down next to the bone. Dust the meat with salt and pepper and rub over with half of the butter. Roast in the oven allowing 20 minutes to the pound. Put the meat aside in a dish to keep warm and keep the meat juices in the roasting pan. In a separate pan melt the rest of the butter, add the shallot, tomato, and the boiled onion. Season to taste and cook until the vegetables are soft. Stir this into the meat juices in the roasting pan, add the cooked beans, heat and pour over the meat.

Moules Marinière

Preparation and cooking time: *1$\frac{1}{2}$ hours*
SERVES 4

1 quart mussels
5 fl.oz. cold water
5 fl.oz. white wine
1 carrot, sliced
1 onion, sliced
2 cloves garlic, crushed
1 bouquet garni
2 oz. [$\frac{1}{4}$ cup] **butter**
salt and pepper
To garnish:
1 tablespoon chopped fresh parsley

Wash and scrub the mussels thoroughly. Put the carrot, onion, garlic, bouquet garni, butter, salt and pepper into a pan with the wine and water. Bring to the boil and simmer for 30 minutes. Strain the liquid into a large pan. Add the mussels to this liquid, cover the pan, and cook over a strong heat shaking the pan constantly. Turn the mussels gently after 5 minutes so that the top ones go to the bottom, and cook for another 5 minutes until all the mussels are open. Discard any mussels that do not open.
Take out the mussels, put them in a deep dish and pour the liquid over them. Sprinkle with parsley, and serve.

Chervil
Potato Soup

Preparation and cooking time: *1 hour*
SERVES 4-6

2 oz. [4 tablespoons] **butter**
$\frac{1}{2}$ lb. **potatoes, peeled and sliced**
1$\frac{1}{2}$ pints [3$\frac{3}{4}$ cups] **water**
salt
5 fl.oz. milk
2 teaspoons chopped fresh chervil

Melt the butter in a pan and cook the potatoes gently for 10 minutes. Add the water and salt and cook for a further 30 minutes. Then strain them off and pass the potatoes through a sieve, or put them into a blender. Heat the milk. Put the potato purée back into the pan, stir in the hot milk and the chervil.
Heat and serve with fried bread croutons.

Creamy, appetising Lovage Soup would make an ideal first course for any dinner party (see recipe on page 40).

Chives
Vichysoisse

This soup is usually served cold but it is also good hot in winter.
Preparation and cooking time:
45 minutes
SERVES 6-8

1 onion, finely chopped
6 leeks, finely chopped
2 oz. [4 tablespoons] butter
1½ pints [3¾ cups] chicken stock
4 or 5 potatoes, peeled and sliced
salt
1 pint [2½ cups] milk
5 fl.oz. cream
nutmeg or mace (optional)
To garnish:
2 tablespoons chopped fresh chives

Sauté the onion and leeks in the butter. Cover and cook slowly for 5-10 minutes. Add the stock, potatoes and salt. When potatoes are cooked pass through a sieve, or put in a blender. Heat the milk with the nutmeg and add to potato mixture.
Chill, then beat and add the cream.
Sprinkle with the chives before serving.

Coriander
Ratatouille

This recipe is for a cold ratatouille, served as a salad.
Preparation and cooking time: *1 hour*
SERVES 4

2 aubergines [eggplant]
salt
2 onions
3 tablespoons olive oil
2 red peppers
4 tomatoes, peeled and chopped
1 clove garlic, sliced
coriander seeds
To garnish:
fresh parsley or basil, chopped

Slice the aubergines, sprinkle salt on them and leave to drain in a colander. Slice the onions and sauté them in a pan with the oil. Seed and chop the red peppers. When the onions are soft add the slices of aubergine and red pepper to the pan. Cover and allow to simmer for 30 minutes. Then add the tomatoes, garlic and about ten coriander seeds, ground. Cook for a further 15 minutes.

Put into a bowl and leave to cool.
When cold sprinkle the ratatouille with chopped parsley or basil.

Dill
Choldnik

This a lovely cold soup for the summer.
Preparation and cooking time:
45 minutes, plus chilling time
SERVES 4

½ lb. turnip or beetroot [beet] tops, or spinach
2 cucumbers
1 pint [2½ cups] stock
2 teaspoons salt
10 fl.oz. sour cream
2 sprigs fresh dill, chopped

Boil the turnip tops or other vegetables in water and drain, then pass them through a sieve or put into a blender. Peel and thinly slice the cucumbers. Add the vegetable purée and the cucumber to the stock, mix well and add the salt. Chill and serve, topped with sour cream and chopped dill.

Dill Potatoes

Preparation and cooking time:
45 minutes
SERVES 2-4

2 lb. potatoes
2 onions, finely chopped
1 clove garlic, crushed
2 fl.oz. oil or butter
2 tablespoons flour
salt
3 tablespoons chopped fresh dill
4 fl.oz. single [light] cream

Boil the potatoes in their skins, then peel and slice them thinly. Sauté the onion and garlic in the oil or butter until golden. Add the flour, then stir in a little cold water. Add salt and dill and simmer for 5 minutes. Add potatoes and re-heat slowly. Put in the cream just before serving.

Fennel
Kidney Savoury

Preparation and cooking time: *½ hour*
SERVES 2

2 oz. [¼ cup] butter
1 clove garlic, sliced
1 onion, chopped
6 lamb kidneys, sliced
5 fl.oz. stock
1 tablespoon flour
½ tablespoon fennel seed
salt and pepper

Melt the butter and sauté the garlic and onion in it. Add the sliced kidneys and the stock. Cook gently for 10-15 minutes, then stir in the flour and fennel seed. Stir until thickened, season to taste and serve on toast.

Garlic
Taramasalata

Tarama is the dried and salted roe of the grey mullet, but, as this is not always readily available, smoked cod roe is usually substituted. If you are buying a whole roe look for a soft one. Potted roes are good, and often of a smoother texture. Serve this with bread or toast and black olives.
Preparation time: *½ hour*.
SERVES 4-6

3 slices white bread
milk
¼ lb. tarama or smoked cod roe
3-4 cloves garlic, crushed or
**   2 tablespoons grated onion**
juice of 1-2 lemons
4 tablespoons olive or corn oil
black pepper

Remove the bread crusts and soak the slices in a little milk. Remove the skin from the roe, and pound the roe in a mortar until it has a creamy consistency. Squeeze the excess milk from the bread. Add the bread and the garlic (or onion, or both) and continue mixing and pounding. When smooth add the lemon juice, oil and black pepper. (The proportions of garlic, oil, and lemon must, of course, be adjusted to personal taste.) Beat the mixture into a cream.

Young Fennel shoots are good eaten as a vegetable (above), and Rosemary will add flavour to chops (right).

Lovage
Lovage Soup

Preparation and cooking time: ¾ hour
SERVES 6-8

2 onions, sliced
1 clove garlic, sliced
1 oz. [2 tablespoons] butter
2 tablespoons chopped fresh lovage
1 oz. [¼ cup] flour
4 large potatoes, peeled and sliced
2 pints [5 cups] stock
salt
10 fl.oz. milk
2 tablespoons chopped fresh parsley

Sauté the sliced onions and garlic in the butter. Add the lovage. Add flour and cook for a few minutes, then add potatoes, stock and salt. Stir until it comes to the boil.
Simmer until potatoes are cooked.
Add milk and put through a sieve or put in a blender.
Reheat and add the chopped parsley before serving.

Marigold Petals
Gold Rice

Preparation and cooking time:
40 minutes
SERVES 4-6

1 onion, finely chopped
sunflower or olive oil
½ lb. [1¼ cups] long grain rice
1 pint [2½ cups] stock
¼ teaspoon salt
pinch of rosemary
½ tablespoon marigold petals
1 oz. [4 tablespoons] cheese, grated
1 oz. [2 tablespoons] butter

Gently fry the onion in the oil and add the rice. Add stock, salt and rosemary and cook until rice is done.
Strain off, reserving half a cup of stock. Put the petals in this hot stock, and add to the rice. Sprinkle with cheese and dot with butter.

Marigold Buns

Preparation and cooking time: ¼ hour
MAKES 12 BUNS

¼ lb. [½ cup] sugar
¼ lb. [½ cup] butter
2 eggs, beaten
½ lb. [2 cups] self-raising flour
handful marigold petals

Heat oven to 350°F (Gas Mark 4, 180°C).
Cream together the sugar and butter. Add the beaten eggs, and fold in the flour and marigold petals. Put in mounds on a greased baking sheet or in cupcake tins, and bake for about 15 minutes.

Marjoram
Austrian Liver

Preparation and cooking time: ½ hour
SERVES 2

2 oz. [¼ cup] cooking fat
1 onion, sliced
1 lb. calf or pig liver, sliced
½ tablespoon chopped fresh marjoram
salt and pepper
1 oz. [¼ cup] flour
4 fl.oz. stock

Heat the fat and fry the onions in it until they are golden. Push the onions to one side of the pan and put in the liver and the marjoram and season with pepper. Fry for about 4 minutes, turning the liver several times. Add salt at the end of the cooking time. Put the onions and liver onto a hot dish. Stir the flour into the fat left in the pan, add the stock, season to taste and cook gently for a few minutes.
Pour the sauce over the liver and onions and serve.

Moussaka

A traditional Greek dish.
Preparation and cooking time: 1½ hours
SERVES 4

3 or 4 aubergines [eggplant]
salt
vegetable oil for frying
2 onions, chopped fine
1½ lb. minced [ground] lamb or beef
pepper
1 teaspoon allspice *or* cinnamon and nutmeg
1 lb. tomatoes, peeled and chopped
3-4 tablespoons chopped fresh marjoram

For the Bechamel Sauce:
1 oz. [2 tablespoons] butter
1 oz. [4 tablespoons] flour
10 fl.oz. milk, hot
1 egg yolk

Heat oven to 350°F (Gas Mark 4, 180°C).
Slice the aubergines, salt them and leave to drain.
Dry the aubergines and fry lightly in oil, drain them on kitchen paper. Fry the chopped onion till golden, add the meat and fry till brown. Add salt and pepper to taste, allspice (or cinnamon and nutmeg), tomatoes and marjoram. Stir well, add a little water or wine and cook for 15 minutes. Put alternate layers of aubergines and the meat mixture in a deep baking dish or wide cake tin.
To make the Bechamel sauce, melt the butter, stir in the flour, add the hot milk slowly and, finally, stir in the egg yolk. Add salt and pepper to taste and cook gently for a few minutes but do not allow to boil. Pour the sauce over the meat and bake for about 45 minutes.

Pork in Cider

Preparation and cooking time: 1½ hours
SERVES 4

4 pieces pork tenderloin *or* 1½-2 lb. other lean pork
2 tablespoons flour, seasoned
vegetable oil for frying
1 clove garlic, chopped
1 onion, chopped
3 teaspoons chopped fresh marjoram
1 bay leaf, crumbled
salt
10 fl.oz. cider

Heat oven to 350°F (Gas Mark 4, 180°C).
Cut the meat into cubes and roll them in the seasoned flour. Put a little oil into a pan, heat it, and quickly brown the meat on all sides to seal in the juices. Remove the meat to a casserole dish. Sprinkle the rest of the ingredients over the meat, and add a little extra salt. Pour in the cider. Cover and bake in the oven for 1 hour.

Stiphado ✳

A tasty, filling dish in which you can use a cheap cut of steak.
Preparation and cooking time: 2½ hours
SERVES 4

2 lb. steak
salt and pepper
2 tablespoons oil
2 lb. small onions
4 cloves garlic, chopped
tomato purée mixed with a little
    water to make 10 fl.oz.
1 glass red wine
1 tablespoon chopped fresh
    marjoram

Cut the steak (chuck will do) into 2-inch cubes. Rub well with salt and pepper. Heat the oil in a stew pan and fry the meat, onions and garlic until meat is browned.
Add the tomato purée, wine and marjoram. Cover very tightly and simmer for 2 hours until the meat is tender and the sauce is thick.

Parsley
Baked Turbot

Preparation and cooking time:
45 minutes
SERVES 4

1 oz. [2 tablespoons] butter
1 small onion, finely chopped
1 tablespoon chopped fresh parsley
4 turbot fillets or other white fish
salt and pepper
2 oz. [⅔ cup] white breadcrumbs
1 wineglass white wine
To garnish:
1 lemon, sliced
parsley sprigs

Heat oven to 350°F (Gas Mark 4, 180°C).
Butter a flat baking dish, with half of the butter. Sprinkle half of the chopped onion and parsley over it and put the fish slices on this. Dot with the remaining butter. Then add the rest of the onion and parsley, and the salt, pepper, and breadcrumbs. Pour on the wine, cover with aluminium foil and bake in the oven for 30 minutes.
Serve garnished with lemon slices and parsley sprigs.

Provencale Tomatoes

Serve this with meat, chicken or fish.
Preparation and cooking time:
30 minutes
SERVES 2-4

2 cloves garlic, crushed
3 tablespoons chopped fresh parsley

2 tablespoons olive oil
4 oz. [1 cup] breadcrumbs
4 large medium-ripe tomatoes

Heat oven to 400°F (Gas Mark 6, 200°C).
Mix together the garlic, parsley, olive oil and breadcrumbs. Cut the tomatoes in half, squeeze gently and shake to remove some of the seeds. Fill them with the breadcrumb mixture. Place the tomatoes on a baking sheet or dish and bake in the oven for 15 minutes.

Sausage and Apple Flan

Preparation and cooking time: *1 hour*
SERVES 4

1 baked 8-inch flan case
10 fl.oz. milk
1 egg, beaten
1 egg yolk
salt and pepper
1 dessert apple, peeled, cored and
    chopped
1 tablespoon chopped fresh parsley
2 pork sausages, partly cooked
    under grill [broiler]
To garnish:
2 tomatoes, sliced
parsley

Heat oven to 375°F (Gas Mark 5, 190°C).
Gently heat the milk to blood heat and pour on beaten egg and yolk. Season well. Stir in chopped apple and parsley. Slice the sausages and arrange in the bottom of the flan case. Pour the egg mixture on the flan.
Bake in the oven for 35 minutes or until sausages are cooked and egg mixture is set.
Garnish with tomato slices and parsley, and serve.

Rosemary
Beef Stew
with Rosemary

Preparation and cooking time: *5½ hours*
SERVES 6

2½-3 lb. chuck steak, shin beef, *or*
    other cheap cut of beef
½ lb. bacon, cut into pieces
4 tomatoes, peeled
3 cloves garlic, sliced
½ teaspoon chopped fresh rosemary
1 glass wine
salt and pepper

Heat oven to 300°F (Gas Mark 2, 150°C).
Put the meat into a casserole. Cover with the bacon and add the other ingredients. Cover and bake in the oven for 4 or 5 hours.

Sage
Sage and Onion Tart

Preparation and cooking time: *1 hour*
SERVES 4

3 medium onions, chopped
1 oz. [2 tablespoons] butter
5 fl.oz. cream or milk
1 egg
1 tablespoon chopped fresh sage
1 teaspoon chopped fresh parsley
¼ lb. bacon, cut into pieces
salt and pepper
½ lb. short crust pastry

Heat oven to 400°F (Gas Mark 6, 200°C).
Melt the butter in a pan and sauté the onions in it until they are soft. Add the other ingredients and mix well. Line a baking tin or pie plate with short crust pastry and fill with the mixture. Bake in the oven for about 20 minutes.

Savory
Broad Beans
with Savory

Preparation and cooking time: *1 hour*
SERVES 4

2 tablespoons oil
1 onion, finely chopped
1 clove garlic, crushed or chopped
1 tablespoon chopped fresh parsley
1 teaspoon chopped fresh savory
½ teaspoon chopped fresh lovage
2 lb. broad beans [lima beans]
1 pint [2½ cups] stock
salt
nutmeg
sour cream

Heat the oil in a pan and sauté the onions and garlic. Add the herbs and the beans. Add stock, salt and nutmeg and cook till tender. Drain off any excess liquid then stir in cream and serve.

Chicken Casserole

Preparation and cooking time: *1 hour*
SERVES 4

4 chicken pieces
2 carrots, chopped
2 cloves garlic, crushed
2 teaspoons chopped fresh parsley
2 teaspoons chopped fresh savory
1½ teaspoons salt
1½ pints [3¾ cups] water
For the sauce:
2 tablespoons butter or oil
¼ lb. mushrooms, sliced
½ teaspoon chopped fresh savory
1 teaspoon chopped fresh parsley
2 oz. [½ cup] flour
1 wineglass white wine
2 tablespoons sour cream
1 tablespoon milk

Cook the chicken in a pan with the carrot, garlic, herbs, salt and water. Remove and bone the chicken and keep warm. Strain and reserve the stock. *To make* the sauce. Heat the fat in a pan and gently sauté the mushrooms and herbs for a few minutes. Add the flour and mix well. Slowly add the wine and reserved chicken stock and cook for about 20 minutes or until the mixture thickens.
Remove from the heat and add the milk and sour cream. Put in the chicken pieces. Serve with rice or noodles.

Sorrel
Sorrel Soup

Preparation and cooking time:
15 minutes
SERVES 4

1 oz. [2 tablespoons] butter
1 handful fresh sorrel leaves, washed and chopped
salt
3 tablespoons single [light] cream
1½ pints [3¾ cups] stock

Melt the butter in a pan. Add the sorrel and cook gently for 4 or 5 minutes. Add salt. Next add the cream and cook gently until thick. Gradually add the stock and heat slowly. Do not allow to boil.

Tarragon
Escalope of Veal

This is ideal to serve at a dinner party, the tarragon giving an unusual flavour to a familiar dish.
Preparation and cooking time:
30 minutes
SERVES 4

4 veal escalopes
½ teaspoon flour, seasoned
3 oz. [6 tablespoons] butter
2 tomatoes, peeled and sliced
¼ lb. mushrooms, wiped and sliced
1 teaspoon chopped fresh tarragon
salt and pepper

Coat the meat in the seasoned flour. Melt two thirds of the butter in a large saucepan. Add the meat and fry on both sides until brown. Remove the meat from the pan and keep warm. Add the remaining butter and fry the tomatoes and mushrooms until soft.
Add the tarragon and the cooked veal. Stir and cook slowly for a further 6-10 minutes. Season to taste and serve.

Tarragon Chicken

This recipe is for casseroled chicken, but a roasting chicken can be given quite a delicious flavour by stuffing it with a mixture of butter and tarragon and basting frequently with the fragrant butter that oozes out during the cooking time.
Preparation and cooking time: *2½ hours*
SERVES 4

2-3 lb. chicken, whole
2 tablespoons chopped fresh tarragon
1 oz. [2 tablespoons] butter
10 fl.oz. stock
1 tablespoon cream

Heat oven to 375 °F (Gas Mark 5, 190 °C).
Rub the chicken with half the tarragon, and put it in a flameproof casserole with the butter and stock. Cover and cook in the oven for 1½ hours or until tender.
Remove the chicken to a serving dish and keep warm.
Add the remaining tarragon to the liquid in the casserole and cook gently for a few minutes on top of the stove, adding the cream. Pour over chicken and serve.

Varda Pork Chops

Serve these chops with boiled rice and a green salad.
Preparation and cooking time: *2¼ hours*
SERVES 4

4 fl.oz. olive oil
4 cloves garlic, crushed
salt and pepper
4 large loin pork chops
1 lb. canned tomatoes
½ tablespoon chopped fresh tarragon

Heat oven to 375 °F (Gas Mark 5, 190 °C).
Heat the oil in a flameproof dish and sauté the garlic. Season the chops with salt and pepper. Put them in the dish and fry on both sides until brown. Add the tomatoes with their liquid and the tarragon. Cover, place in the oven and cook for 1¼-1½ hours.

Thyme
Meat Loaf

Preparation and cooking time: *1½ hours*
SERVES 4

1 oz. [¼ cup] breadcrumbs
1 lb. steak, minced [ground]
½ lb. bacon, minced
1 onion, chopped
1 teaspoon chopped fresh thyme
salt and pepper
1 egg
5 fl.oz. milk

Heat oven to 350 °F (Gas Mark 4, 180 °C).
Mix together the breadcrumbs, steak, bacon, onion, thyme, salt and pepper. Add the egg and milk and mix well. Put in a greased loaf tin and cover with foil. Bake in the oven for 1 hour, or until cooked but firm.

Chicken with Tarragon, Baked Basil Tomatoes, Potatoes with Parsley and, for dessert, Pears with Sweet Cicely— this meal makes full use of herbs.

herbs for beauty

Herbs have been used for cosmetic purposes since before Biblical times. Unfortunately, however, they were largely superseded by mass-produced cosmetics and only recently are people beginning to rediscover the goodness and exhilarating effects of the old herbal products—many of which are as effective, and most of which are certainly purer, than the cosmetics you can buy.

As life gets more and more complicated and technical a reaction in favour of the natural remedies and confections is, not unexpectedly, taking place. Herbs are staging a great come-back in every way. Herbs in beauty are, however, only a small part of herbs in life. There is little point in washing in Elderflower water and rinsing your hair in Rosemary if you spend the rest of your life eating frozen or fried foods. The use of herbs and good fresh vegetables in food is as important to beauty and good looks as the use of them in cosmetics—it is all part of the same thing.

Many of the herbal beauty aids can be bought direct from herbalists, but some you can easily make up yourself.

Herbs to put in the bath

Herbs added to a bath are refreshingly fragrant, and it is often much nicer to pick and add fresh leaves or flowers to your bath rather than rely upon the mass-produced, chemical mixtures you can buy.

How you add the herbs is really a matter of choice. You could add an infusion, (made in the same way as a herb tea, see p.23); a few drops of oil (see p.26); a scattering of leaves or petals just dropped into the water—although with some things, pine or fir twigs for example, this might be uncomfortable; alternatively you could put the herbs into a little muslin bag and hang the bag under the hot water tap so that the water running over it releases the fragrance of the herbs.

Lovage is one of the best herbs to add to a bath, either in an infusion put into the water, or the leaves put into a bag through which the hot water can run.

This has great tonic and deodorant qualities.

For a tonic spring bath chop a mixture of dried Nettle, Dandelion, Daisy and Cowslip, infuse it in hot water for half an hour, then strain off and add the hot liquid to the bath. Another good bath mixture is made from Pine, Larch, Fir and Juniper twigs, infused in the same way.

An infusion of Angelica leaves in the bath is a good skin stimulant. And other herbs which are marvellous added to a bath are Basil, Camomile, Elder flowers, and, of course, Lavender.

Herbs for hair

Herbal hair rinses are very easy to make—basically they are a cold tea—and they are good for all sorts of things —to clear dandruff, to lighten or darken hair and, of course, as a general conditioner to bring out the highlights in the hair.

Infusions of Lime flowers or Nettles make good hair conditioners if used as a final rinse. If an infusion of Parsley is rubbed into the hair and scalp every few days it is said to help clear dandruff. An infusion of Rosemary made in the usual way—pour boiling water over two or three sprigs of rosemary, let it cool, and warm it up again just before use—not only makes the hair smell wonderful but it is extremely good for it and will darken dark hair. Use it as a final rinse. An infusion of Camomile flowers used in the same way will brighten fair hair. Rumour related that Lucrezia Borgia used some 'unnatural means' to lighten her hair—blondes being unusual in Italy—perhaps her secret concoction was nothing more ominous than infusion of Camomile.

Face packs

Face packs are cleansing and stimulating for the skin. Yoghurt with an infusion of Fennel seeds and some chopped Fennel leaves is a tonic and wrinkle smoother. A pack of white of egg and lemon with some finely chopped Yarrow helps to clear spots and is good for a greasy skin. And Elderflowers mixed with yoghurt make a tonic face pack.

Spread these face packs on evenly, avoiding the eyes and mouth, and leave them for about 10-15 minutes. Then rinse off with lukewarm water. As with any face pack, be careful not to laugh or screw up your face while they are on. This disturbs or cracks the pack and detracts from its beneficial effect. Once a week or so is often enough to use them.

Creams

Any plain unscented cold cream can be easily turned into a fragrant herbal cream. You can just add chopped herb leaves to the cream—but you may find it difficult to remove the little pieces of herb from your face! Alternatively, heat the cold cream up gently in a pan and add a little herb oil (made according to the method on page 26) to it.

Cleansers and washes

Face washes are, again, basically cold teas. They are infusions of herbs, made in the usual way, which are then patted onto the skin with a ball of cotton wool. All of them are refreshing, and some have particularly beneficial effects.

To clear the skin and, according to some hopeful people, to take away freckles pour boiling water over a handful of Elderflowers and their leaves in late spring, and wash the face night and morning with a pad of cotton wool dipped in the cooled liquid.

The leaves of the Dead-nettle made into an infusion make a mildly astringent face lotion. And other good face washes can be made with Lemon Balm and with Lime flowers. This last one is reputed to be good for wrinkles.

Yarrow is a herb full of good qualities. The leaves and flowers are gathered in early summer and a tea is made which is both drunk and applied externally to the face as a cleaner and beautifier which is particularly good for greasy skins. A teaspoon of the fresh or dried herb per cup with boiling water makes the tea. (And Yarrow is also useful to add to a bath.)

Eye Lotions

A tea or infusion (see p.23) of Verbena, Fennel, Elderflowers, or Eyebright (this is the best one, not surprisingly in view of its name) left to get cold, makes a mild eye bath. These eye-baths are restoring to tired eyes and helpful in cases of conjunctivitis and eye strain.

Feet

Foot baths can really help tired and aching feet. Try an infusion of Lavender, Lime flowers or Marigold leaves added to a foot bath. The fragrance floating upwards will revive you, while the fragrant water is reviving your feet.

Face washes, creams, hair rinses—you can make many beauty preparations with herbs. A Camomile hair rinse (right) is particularly good for fair hair.

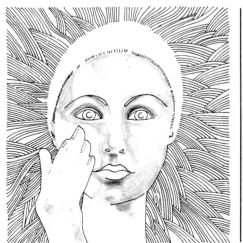

Use a Rosemary hair rinse (top left). Three stages in thé use of a face pack (left). First, apply the pack evenly being careful not to put any too near to your eyes or mouth. Next, leave the pack for ten minutes or so to harden and then rinse it off with luke-warm water.

Rose petals perfume a bath (top right). Herbs tied into a cotton or muslin bag and hung under the hot water tap will release their fragrance and perfume your bath (right), while eye washes made from infusions of herbs will refresh tired eyes.

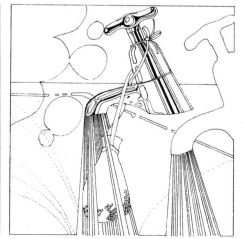
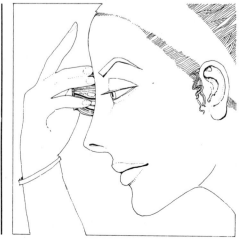

gifts to make from herbs

If you grow your own herbs you can make many beautiful, yet inexpensive, gifts— Lavender bags, jars of pot pourri and herb pillows and sachets in different shapes and sizes.

The most simple gifts are often the most welcome—particularly when the recipient knows you have made them yourself—and there are countless things which you can make very easily from the herbs and flowers grown in your own garden, or gathered from the countryside. Dried herbs in decorative glass jars, pots of herbal cream, even a flourishing pot of Basil—all of these make delightful presents to give or to keep for yourself.

Herb pillows

Herb cushions were used in Victorian days to soothe the nerves and to induce a refreshing sleep. And the clean, fresh scent of a little Lavender cushion tucked behind the head was then held to be an excellent cure for the vapours! When put under the pillows of insomniacs these little herb pillows really can help to induce sleep.

The simplest way to make a herb pillow is to make a little cotton or linen bag to the size you require and fill this with a mixture of soporific and sweet smelling herbs. Make slip-covers for these pillows—remembering that it is advisable to use a fabric which launders easily—either in gay bold stripes or patterns or, perhaps, in a pretty sprigged print.

Use dried herbs to fill the pillow. Equal quantities of Lavender, Lemon Verbena and Peppermint make an excellent sweet-smelling base. And for a sleep-inducing pillow add small quantities of any of the following—all of which are pleasantly scented and will blend well together:

Angelica
Bergamot
Dill
Hops
Lemon Balm
Marjoram
Rosemary
Sage
Thyme

Other fragrant mixtures are:
a mixture of equal parts of Rosemary blossoms, Rosemary leaves, Pine needles, Rose Geranium leaves, and Lemon Balm; or a mixture of equal parts of Rose Geranium leaves and Thyme with double that amount of Lavender and of Rose petals.
Lastly here is an ancient recipe for 'A Bag to Smell Unto for Melancholy or to cause one to Sleep'.
'Take dry Rose leaves, put in a glass jar, powder dried Mint leaves and add ground Cloves, and mix with the Rose leaves. Put in a bag under the pillow

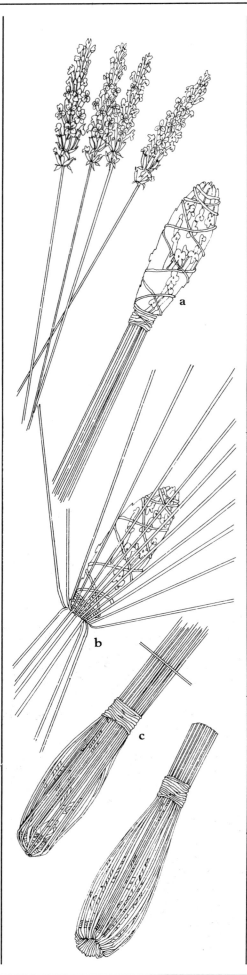

and this will cause sleep, and is pleasant to smell when awake.'

Herb Sachets

Smaller bags including the herbs used in the pillows not only scent cupboards and drawers, they also help to keep moths away. A dried stalk or two of Southernwood is very good against moths and will add a subtle aromatic scent. And it is pleasant to think of this ancient herb being used in the same way it was in medieval times when its French name was *Garderobe*.

Make a sachet to fit the shelf in a drawer or linen cupboard and fill it with a thin layer of Lemon Verbena, or Lavender, and you will always have sweet smelling bed linen. Lemon Verbena is a delicious herb and its citrious fragrance will keep the linen cupboard fresh, while the linen will hold a slightly lemony tang.

You can also make herbal handkerchief sachets and stocking bags. Put a small layer of herbs between the lining and the top covering material, and to stop all the herbs falling to the bottom of the bag or sachet stitch through the two layers of material in a quilting pattern. A thoughtful gift idea for someone who has to live out of a suitcase a lot of the time is a travel sachet. These can be made of cotton or gingham, and should contain a thin layer of Pot-Pourri or Lavender. Bear in mind that it must lie flat in the bottom of a suitcase and be as light as possible.

Here is one suggestion for a mixture to put into scented sachets:
equal parts of Southernwood, Bergamot, and Lemon Balm with twice that amount of Rose petals and twice as much again of Lavender. A few crushed Coriander seeds, Cloves or Cinnamon can be added to the herbs and petals.

Lavender bundles

These make an attractive alternative to sachets and have long been popular among people who grow their own lavender. They are very easy to make, but you must use freshly-picked Lavender. If it is dry and brittle the stalks will break instead of bending.

Pick long-stemmed sprigs of Lavender on a hot summer's day (so that there is no danger of it being damp). Arrange it with all the heads neatly next to each other and then bind them together with silk or thread (see diagram a) finishing off by binding tightly just below the heads.

Next bend the stalks back just below the thread and bring them over so that they enclose the flower-heads (see diagram b). It is important that the stalks are evenly arranged and completely cover the heads or when the Lavender dies the flowers will break off and fall out.

Bind thread around tightly just below the bulge of the enclosed flower heads (see diagram c) and, finally, trim the ends of the stalks so that they are even.

Pot Pourri

The sweet fresh scents of summer are captured all the year round in Pot Pourri. This is very easy to make, and is a marvellous present. Simply dry the herbs very carefully using the slower method (see pp 18–19) and then mix them according to your taste. There are many well-loved recipes for Pot Pourris which have been treasured and exchanged down the years. Each is different, and you can experiment with your own mixtures, but—to give you some ideas—here are a few guides.

A simple Pot Pourri:
1 quart rose petals
1 pint Rose Geranium leaves
1 pint Lavender flowers
1 cup Rosemary needles
2 tablespoons each of:
    Ground Cloves
    Cinnamon
    Allspice

Fixative:
3 tablespoons crushed Orris root and powdered Gum Benzoin
20 drops Rose oil
5 drops Heliotrope oil (optional)

(You can buy these from a good herbalist or chemist.)
Dry the rose petals (preferably Damask or Centifolia roses) and the leaves on a flat paper, turning them every day. Put the mixed flowers and leaves into a bowl in layers with the spices. Then add the fixative and run your hands through the Pot pourri to make sure the fixatives are well mixed with the petals, leaves and spices. Mix well and press down, covering the bowl.
Keep it in a dark, dry place.

A Herb Pot-Pourri

This should be made in a bowl or wide jar with a lid so that when the bowl is not in use it can be covered and stored in a dark place to conserve the scents for as long as possible. This Pot Pourri is made from scented leaves, flowers and spices. You choose your own mixture according to what you have growing or can acquire from friends. All the leaves are, of course, dried.

The leaves to be chosen from:
Angelica
Basil
Bay
Bergamot
Borage
Lemon Balm
Lemon Verbena or Thyme
Lovage
Marjoram
Mint
Rosemary
Sage
Sweet Cicely
Tarragon

The flowers to be chosen from:
Borage
Camomile
Elder
Lavender
Lime
Marigold petals
Nasturtium
Rose petals
Violets

Extra scent will be given by all or some of the following:
Cardamom (ground)
Cinnamon
Cloves
Nutmeg

Put the flowers, leaves and spices in layers in the container. The top layer should be very decorative with, perhaps, dried whole rosebuds, pansies and cornflowers among it. Or you could use those flowers which were once considered herbs—Peonies and Honeysuckle.

A Special Pot-Pourri

This is a more complicated affair which uses the petals and buds of about 50 roses!
Pick the roses on a dry day early in the morning but when there is no dew. Spread the petals out in a cool, airy place and turn them every day until they are papery dry. When they are dry put them, mixed with a slightly smaller quantity of salt, into a glass or earthenware jar with a lid. Stir every day for about a week. In the meantime, gather a mass of scented leaves and flowers, about a handful of each, and put them to dry on sheets of paper in a cool dry place.

Some leaves and flowers to choose from and add to would be:
Bay leaves
Carnation or Pink flowers or petals
Scented Geranium leaves
Honeysuckle
Jasmine
Lavender flowers
Lemon Balm
Lemon Verbena
Rosemary leaves
Violets
Wallflowers

When these are dry add them to the rose petal and salt mixture. Next gather together the following:
4 oz. Orris root powder
½ oz. oil of Geranium
½ oz. oil of Lavender
1 oz. ground Coriander seed
1 oz. ground Nutmeg
1 oz. Cloves (whole)
3 Cinnamon sticks

Put some of the Orris powder into a bowl and add the oils, stirring well with all the rest and leave for three weeks to a month stirring from time to time. If the Pot Pourri seems to be becoming too dry, add a little more salt, and if too damp add more Orris root powder.
The spices should retain their strong scent for years, so you can always add more dried flowers another year. This can be put into bowls and set around the house, or given as a present.

Lavender Pot Pourri

Bowls of Lavender in a room are quite delightful and are still used by country women to keep their homes fresh and sweet.
Gather the Lavender when it is in full flower, early in the morning before the sun has reached it, and allow to dry naturally in the sun. Dried Lavender flowers will remain fragrant for years.

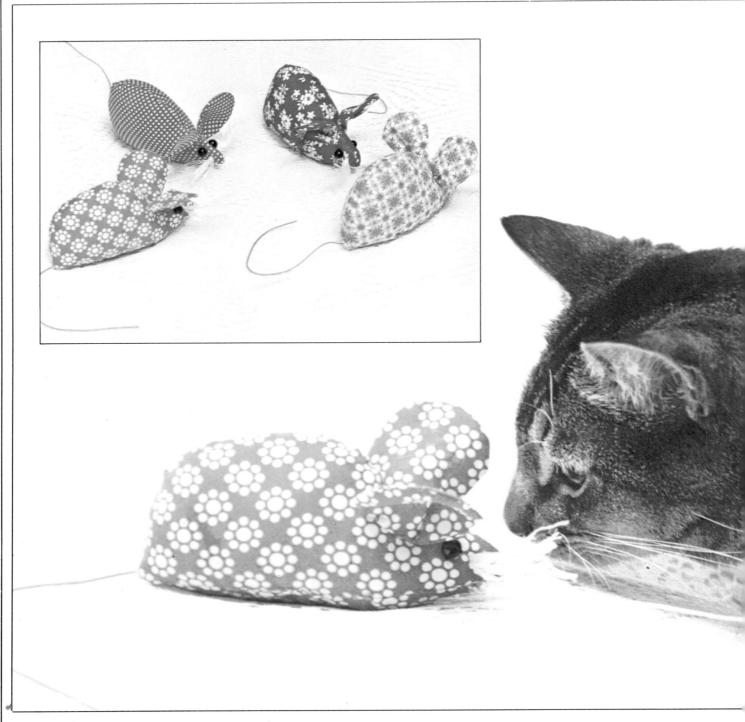

Catnip Mice

While on the subject of herb pillows and sachets remember that there is no better present for a cat than a little pillow or cotton mouse stuffed with dried Catnip (Catmint). Cats adore this plant as anyone who has both a cat and a Catnip plant knows.

How to make a
catnip mouse

Materials
6 inches x 10 inches of mini-printed
   cotton fabric
Matching thread
Catnip, dried and crumbled
4 inches of coloured string
3 inches of fairly thick colourless
   nylon string
2 small round black beads

To cut out:
Trace pattern and cut two sides, one base and two ear pieces.

Making up:
With right sides of fabric together fold one earpiece along the line AB. Seam around earpiece leaving gap. Turn right side out and press. Close seam gap by hand. Repeat for second earpiece. With right sides of fabric together, seam two sides together from C to D to E. Clip seam allowances. Seam the base to the sides from CF to G to HE to I, then leave a gap for stuffing (I to J) and seam from J to CF. Clip seam allowance and turn right side out. Make a big knot at one end of the coloured string, thread the other through a bodkin and draw the string

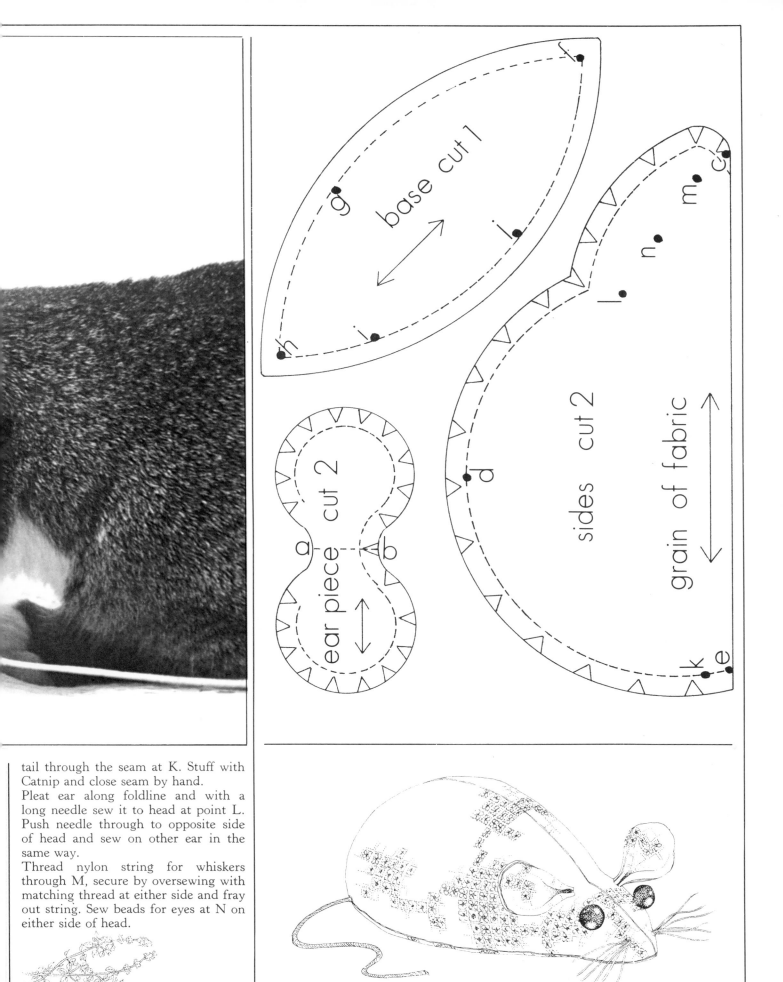

tail through the seam at K. Stuff with Catnip and close seam by hand.

Pleat ear along foldline and with a long needle sew it to head at point L. Push needle through to opposite side of head and sew on other ear in the same way.

Thread nylon string for whiskers through M, secure by oversewing with matching thread at either side and fray out string. Sew beads for eyes at N on either side of head.

base cut 1

sides cut 2

grain of fabric

ear piece cut 2

herbs throughout history

Herbs have always been highly prized for their culinary and medicinal properties. In pre-Roman times, most people lived chiefly on bread and other grain foods, and had meat when—and if—they were lucky. The only way they could give their meals any variety or savour was through the addition of any plants they found growing wild. And so, from necessity and through experiment, trial and error, they gradually learned a tremendous amount about those plants which came to be called herbs. Their knowledge sometimes became interwoven with what is regarded now as superstition. But even when disguised in the form of the most curious beliefs their plant lore still flourished and was often sound.

Herbal knowledge and beliefs were, from the very beginning, gathered together and handed down. And a papyrus has been discovered which shows that in 2000 BC there were more than 2000 herb doctors in Ancient Egypt. The Egyptians gave this knowledge to the Greeks, who passed it on to the Romans.

By the time the Romans were making themselves rulers of the world, they depended so much on herbs for cooking and medicine that the Roman armies carried herbs in their baggage on campaigns and journeys. These they seem to have planted everywhere—sometimes intentionally, sometimes unintentionally.

Rome fell from power, but people went on collecting, growing and using herbs because they needed them for food flavourings and for scent. When the weather became bitterly cold they slaughtered most of their livestock because there was no way of feeding all of them throughout the winter. But it was also difficult to preserve meat successfully. Even when salted it often went rank, and was usually unappetising, so herbs were added to give flavour. And because there was no plumbing or sanitation their clothes and their houses could not be kept fresh and clean. So, again, they needed the strong herbal scents.

Over the centuries agricultural methods, hygiene and sanitation all improved but right up to the eighteenth century and longer herbs were of vital importance in cooking, in medicine, and for general household use.

In the pages that follow the herbs have been put into various groups—Ceremonial herbs, Herbs for fragrance and beauty, and so on—according to their foremost qualities, but almost every one of them had many uses, from the magical to the practical.

The growth of the herb garden

The first planned herb gardens, as opposed to patches of herbs, were in the castles and monastery courtyards. These early gardens were very beautiful because a number of plants now grown for beauty and scent were then counted as herbs. Gillyflowers, Roses, Lilies, Periwinkles, Peonies, Foxgloves and Honeysuckle were all used for sweetmeats or drinks, salads or cosmetics.

Then, too, as honey was the only sweetener some herbs were planted with a secondary view to attracting bees. Or, alternatively, Savory, Thyme, Rosemary, Lavender or Lemon Balm were planted by the hives to flavour the honey.

By the mid-sixteenth century herbs were grown in a widespread way, not only raised in the gardens of castles and monasteries. (In England, in any case, Henry VIII had ordered the dissolution of the monasteries in 1530s.) Herb gardens may now be thought of as nostalgic, ornamental places, but for people who then cultivated them they were as ordinary and as useful as a plot of vegetables.

In the sixteenth century, too, the form of the herb garden changed. The early gardens had been planned strictly for utility. They had been laid out with small, rather empty, rectangular beds, with plenty of walking and picking room between them. This gave the gardens a formal pattern. Then, with the building of comfortable, large houses this formal pattern became more and more complicated and was designed to be seen from the first floor windows of the new, large houses, or from the terraces which encircled them. This change of viewpoint, the garden now being seen from above, made popular the Knot Garden. The simplest of these took the form of a wheel, the spokes being made of compact bulky herbs—Hyssop, Rue, Thyme —the segments between being filled with the shorter herbs. In general, however, the knots were very complicated formal scroll patterns made of lines and curves of miniature hedges, clipped shrubs or herbs—Box and Lavender were popular—and the spaces filled with herbs, ornamental flowers, and sometimes even coloured gravel.

The Herbalists

Herbals, which list the practical uses of plants, have been written since the times of the Romans and before. In fact, many of the herbals written during the Middle Ages drew upon manuscripts dating back to the Dioscorides and Pliny the Elder.

In 1475 Konrad von Megenberg brought out *Das Buch der Natur* which included the first known wood cuts used for botanical illustrations. However, before the sixteenth century very few original illustrations were prepared for herbals—they were all very stylized copies of copies, and came to bear little or no resemblance to the living plant.

Probably the best known herbal is the one written by John Gerard in 1597. Gerard was born in Nantwich, Cheshire, England in 1545 and died in London in 1612. During his lifetime he was a surgeon, the superintendent of Lord Burghley's gardens (Lord Burghley was Elizabeth I's Chief Secretary of State) and an apothecary to James I. One of the illustrations in his herbal is of the potato plant, recently imported from the New World—and is thought to be the first published drawing of it.

John Parkinson, who was 20 years younger than Gerard, was also an apothecary to James I. Parkinson had a famous garden at Longacre, London and in 1640 published his great herbal 'Theatrum Botanicum'.

The herbal which makes particularly fascinating reading is that published by Nicholas Culpeper in 1649. Culpeper linked herbs with astrology and tended to exaggerate the medicinal claims to be made for each plant. His herbal includes a lot of fanciful or superstitious material and also unconcernedly flatly contradicts Gerard and Parkinson.

The frontispiece and some of the illustrations from Gerard's Herbal, published in 1597, together with (centre bottom) a portrait of Gerard himself.

THE
HERBALL
OR GENERALL
Historie of
Plantes.

Gathered by John Gerarde
of London Master in
CHIRVRGERIE.

Imprinted at London by
Iohn Norton.
1597

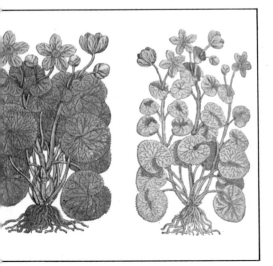

By the mid-seventeenth century the goodwife's guides and recipe books would be found in all kitchens or still-room shelves—Gerard's Herbal; The Profitable Art of Gardening, written by Thomas Hill in 1568; The Good Housewife's Jewel and Rare Conceits in Cookery, written by T. Dawson in 1585, and many others. These books gave the housewife all she needed to know about what hedges to plant— Sweet Briar and Elder—and when; and which seeds to sow when the moon was waxing and cut back when the moon was waning. Other useful information included how to catch moles, how to strengthen seeds by sprinkling them with wine, and how to keep adders out of the garden by planting Wormwood, Mugwort and Southernwood in the corners. (But, on the other hand, adders loved Fennel so care was needed.)

Herbs in cooking

Herbs, above all, have always been a vital ingredient in cooking. For centuries, Mint has given its savour to lamb and mutton, Sage to the greasy flesh of pork and goose, and Dill has made the digestion of foods like cabbage and cucumber much easier.

Before the great explorers and adventurers of the Elizabethan age discovered the New World, and before the great Dutch East India Company (founded 1602) made possible the import of tea and oriental spices, herbs were the only source of tea and of food flavourings. And even after this herbs long continued to be used by most people since the new imports to Europe were extremely expensive. Tea, for example, in England in the mid-seventeenth century cost between six and ten pounds sterling (about 15 to 25 dollars) for one pound in weight!

Almost every herb, regardless of its secondary use for medicine, or perfume, is used in cooking. (See pp 20-21 for a list of herbs and their uses in cooking).

Ceremonial herbs

The herbs listed below are a few of those which played an important part in religion, ritual or tradition.

Bay. The Greeks made Bay into crowns of honour for their poets and heroes. This tradition, linked with the botanical name, *Lauris Nobilis*, has come down the centuries as far as twentieth-century Britain in the idea of the 'Poet Laureate'.

Bay was sacred to Apollo, the sun god, and, belonging to the sun, was a strong defence against evil and the powers of

L HERBORISTE

darkness, Where a Bay tree grew, no witch or devil, thunder or lightning could do harm. At Delphi, the Oracle and the lesser priestesses spoke their prophecies with a Bay leaf between their lips, perhaps to keep all harm or evil from their words.

Coriander. This is a very ancient herb, for Coriander seeds have been found in tombs of the twenty-first Egyptian dynasty (1085-945 BC).

It is spoken of, too, in the Old Testament of the Bible. When the Children of Israel were returning to their homeland from slavery in Egypt, they ate manna in the wilderness, and 'the manna was as Coriander seed'. It is still one of the traditional 'Bitter Herbs' to be eaten at the Passover, when the Jewish people remember their great journey.

Elder. There is a tradition that the cross on which Christ was crucified was made of Elder wood. Perhaps because of this, people believed that Elder possessed a great power against evil and black magic, but although they valued it, they feared it, too. They thought it an unlucky wood from which to make cradle rockers because the spirit of the tree might harm the child. Farmers were unwilling to use an Elder switch to drive cattle. And one legend held that the tree would only grow where blood had been shed.

Hyssop. This was a holy herb, used in purification ceremonies in the temples of many countries including the Temple of Solomon. In one of the psalms of King David there is the prayer 'Purge me with Hyssop and I shall be clean.' Hyssop was held to have the power to cleanse away evil, and so, naturally enough, it found an everyday use, too, in the Middle Ages, when it was used as a strewing herb to give freshness and cleanliness to a house.

Herbs for fragrance and beauty

In the middle ages plants like Thyme, Lavender, Mint, Basil, and Hyssop were used for strewing on the bare or straw-covered floors of houses, while for the floors of churches special herbs —Marjoram and Rosemary—were used. Up until the eighteenth century, while there was little personal hygiene and less sanitation, plants from the herb garden were made into pot-pourri and sweet-scented posies (tussie mussies) to ward off the foul smells that were everywhere, indoors and out. While for those who could enjoy the rare luxury of being clean, there were herbal bath essences, hair rinses and tooth washes. Oils from the seeds of herbs were used, from Roman until Tudor times, for polishing wooden floors and furniture. Below are listed some of the most important of the fragrant herbs.

Camomile. In Tudor England Camomile was used in the Knot Gardens, and for lawns as a substitute for grass. There is a story that Francis Drake was playing bowls on a Camomile lawn when the Spanish Armada was sighted.

Because of its sweet scent when dried, Camomile was used for strewing on bare floors and for beauty preparations —being made into a kind of shampoo.

Lavender. This is one of the most famous of all herbs, but there is little record of it in England until the middle of the sixteenth century. It is, however, fairly certain that the Romans brought it with them to Britain as they used it to perfume their baths. (Its name, *Lavandula Officinalis* in fact, comes from the Latin *lavare*, to wash.) Lavender was probably grown in monastery gardens, but its lack of medical usefulness kept it in the background. Then, in Tudor times, people rediscovered its fragrance, and its power to ease stiff joints and relieve tiredness, and it was brought in quantities from herb farms to the London Herb Market at Bucklersbury. 'Who'll buy my Lavender?' became perhaps the most famous of all the London street-cries. And in France, now as in the seventeenth century, huge fields of Lavender are grown for the perfume trade.

Meadowsweet. Queen of the Meadows. Tradition said that this was a sacred plant to the Druids, and certainly it was much used as a strewing herb. John Gerard thought very warmly of it: 'The leavs and floures farr excell all other strong herbs, for to deck up houses, to straw in chambers, halls, and banqueting houses in Summer time; for the smell thereof makes the heart merrie, delighteth the senses…'. And it was said, too, that 'Queene Elizabeth of famous memory, did more desire it than any other herb to strew her chambers withall.'

Nettle. One species is known as Roman nettle, so it is likely that the Romans used it both as a vegetable and a herb. Apart from enjoying the young shoots as a spring vegetable, people found that eating them was good for the complexion. This would certainly still be a very inexpensive way of keeping a good skin, so it may be worth trying.

Rosemary. This is a herb that has a place in almost every one of the groups within the great herb family. One of the many legends about it tells that its blue flowers were once white but that when the Holy Family fled into Egypt, the Virgin Mary spread her cloak on a Rosemary bush, and the blossoms turned blue in her honour. Another story was that the plant will grow in height for 33 years, the length of Christ's life, and then grow no taller. And a much more earthly view was that where Rosemary flourishes, the wife rules!

Rosemary had many uses. Its invigorating scent warded off pestilence (and black magic) and made it a substitute for incense. When it was put into the fire used for cooking, it made a lovely smell. It soothed headaches and stimulated the heart. It was (and is) good for the hair and skin. And finally, it was the herb of fidelity, worn by bride and bridegroom at their wedding.

Southernwood. This plant's French name was 'Garderobe' and it was much used in medieval France in its dried form to hang in clothes cupboards and chests to give a lovely scent and to keep the moth away. It was widely grown, too, in Elizabethan gardens, and often picked for the pleasure of its perfume. One of its country names, Lad's Love, came about because it was so often put into the posies which lovers gave to their sweethearts, partly for its scent, and partly because it was believed to be a love charm. The same two reasons made it a favourite strewing herb for bedrooms.

Woodruff. This is another herb which was popular in the fourteenth and fifteenth centuries for its perfume, and hung in rooms and linen presses. John Gerard recommended it to be used indoors to 'attemper the air, coole and make fresh the place…' It was strewn over floors, too, and put inside mattresses, and on special occasions was used to decorate churches.

Thyme. To the Greeks Thyme was a symbol of courage. They used it in baths and for strewing, while its antiseptic quality made it favoured as an incense in temples and theatres. And the Romans burnt it in their rooms.

THE GROUNDSEL MAN

Herbs in magic and myth

Obviously, herbs, which were so valuable to people and could even sometimes mean the difference between life and death, played a great part in magic and superstition. Astrology was used to work out the most propitious times for the planting and harvesting of herbs. Certain of them were thought to be under the influence of a particular planet—Chives, for example, belonged to Mars, and Chervil to Jupiter—and the position of the sun and moon were also taken into account when planning to sow or harvest. Even today, just to be on the safe side, many people still plant herbs during the waxing of the moon. Because people knew the power and usefulness of herbs in their everyday life, they turned to them for help against evil and harmful magic. They believed, for example, that Rosemary, Lavender, Dill, Hyssop, Angelica and Southernwood would protect them from witchcraft and the evil eye. The leaves of the Elder were gathered on the last day of April and fixed around doors and windows and it was believed that the inhabitants would then be in no danger from the charms and spells of witches. The Elder was a magic tree, all herbs were under the protection of the Elder Mother and, although it was full of love for mankind, it was wiser to ask its pardon if forced to cut it.

Basil. This is a herb of contradictions. In Western Europe it has been thought both to belong to the Devil and to be a sovereign remedy against witches. The Greeks and Romans believed that people must curse when they sowed Basil to ensure germination. There was even a doubt about whether it was poisonous or not, and one record claimed that 'Hollerius, a French physitian, affirms…that an acquaintance of his by common smelling to it had a Scorpion bred in his brain'.

Lady's Mantle. Lady's Mantle was a special dew flower because drops collected in the cup of the grey-green leaves. And dew, especially dew in May, had a magical power to preserve a woman's youth, and took extra value from the Plant where it was found. Whoever collected the dew had to go out alone, in full moonlight, naked and with bare feet as a sign of purity to ward off any lurking evil forces.

Marjoram. The name Marjoram means 'Joy of the Mountain'. According to Greek myth, Amarakos was a youth in the service of the king of Cyprus. One day he dropped a jar of perfume, and fainted in terror, and the gods changed him into Marjoram. Venus herself was the first to grow it, and when it grew on a tomb, it was believed that all was well with the dead.

Marigold. The Greeks delighted in Marigolds for decoration. In medieval times they were an emblem of love, and had a main part in at least one complicated spell which would enable a young maiden to discover whom she would marry. To dream of them was a sign of all good things, and simply to look at them drove away evil humours.

Mint. Legend has it that Menthe was a nymph whom Pluto, the lord of the Underworld, loved. Pluto's wife, Proserpine, was jealous of her so turned her into the herb which bears her name.

For the Greeks Mint was a magic herb, used in their mysteries and probably, too, in their perfumes and baths. In Athens people scented different parts of their bodies with different herbs, and Mint was kept for the arms, to give them the smell of strength.

Mugwort. Astrologers regarded Mugwort as a plant of Venus, and therefore useful for treating women's ailments. If it was picked on St. John's Day, it gave protection against misfortune, ill-health and weariness.

The Roman writer, Pliny, who compiled the 27 volumes of his *Natural History* in the first century AD was of the opinion that 'They that travel, if they carry Mugwort, will never tire.' He also believed they would never be attacked by wild animals.

Parsley. The god, Hercules, is said to have chosen Parsley for his garlands. The Greeks consequently thought highly of it and wove it into the crowns for victors in the athletic games.

Parsley is very slow to germinate, and the magical explanation for this was that before it came up it had to go to the devil and back seven times. People believed, too, that only a witch could grow it, and that a fine harvest was only sure if the seeds were planted on Good Friday, or by a pregnant woman.

Once planted, Parsley was not to be moved. Change displeased it and that could bring misfortune to the household.

Rue. In ancient times, Rue was very potent. The god Mercury gave it to Odysseus to set him free from the charms of the witch, Circe.

The Greeks believed that Rue stolen from a neighbour's garden throve better than a plant acquired honestly. Even animals were thought to use its power: 'When Weesel is to fight with Serpent, she armeth herself by eating Rue, against the might of the Serpent.' Presumably she then won!

Violet. A Greek myth relates that Zeus fell in love with the beautiful maiden, Io, and turned her into a cow to protect her from the jealous anger of Juno, his wife. The earth grew Violets to be Io's food, and the flower was named after her.

Violets have always been the emblem of modesty, and John Gerard loved them because 'They stirre up a man to that which is comely and honest...'

Herbs in medicine

Herbs were, until comparatively recently, the major source of medicine for when antibiotics and all the other modern drugs were unknown, people were forced to rely upon natural tried and tested cures. The Anglo-Saxon word for plant was 'wort' and plants were named for specific medicinal properties they were held to have. Thus Agrimony was known as Liverwort, Coltsfoot as Coughwort, and so on. Later the common names, many of them sadly no longer used, were more explicit—Yarrow for example was called Nosebleed.

Herbal medicine has, of course, never disappeared. There are still homeopathic pharmacies and certainly people still use traditional herbal cures. In China there have grown up two entirely separate schools of medicine, one centred around modern Western drugs and surgical techniques and the other based upon acupuncture and traditional, mainly herbal, medicines—some of which have remained virtually unchanged for 2,700 years. Recently, too, in the West there has been a drift back to 'natural' cures and herbal medicines in reaction against the ever-increasing complexity of modern drugs.

Medicinal teas
The various herb teas are really the safest, easiest and best ways of getting the benefit from aromatic leaves and flowers of herbs (see page 23). The majority of these teas are also anti-indigestive and relaxing—making them good to drink last thing at night.

The herb teas are believed to have other, more important medical properties, too. Eyebright and Fennel for example, are held to be good for the eyes. Lady's Mantle (called the Alchemist's Herb) makes a tea which is supposedly good for acne and for many peculiarly female conditions. Lemon Balm tea is said to prolong life. Lovage tea is sometimes claimed to act as a deodorant. And a tea made from Woodruff is said to relieve headaches and migraine.

Herbal Medicines
Making your own medicines can be a complicated and somewhat hazardous occupation because many of the herbs have dangerous or unexpected side-effects. So anyone interested would be wise not to attempt it but to investigate the stock of the nearest herbal or homeopathic supplier. Among other things a number of creams and ointments are made from herbs, one well known one being Comfrey ointment which has quite amazingly good effects in cases of back strain. (In medieval times this herb was called Boneset, and recommended for sprains and strained backs.)

Herbal medicine becomes further confused because each herb was used to cure innumerable ailments. Rue, for example, which is dangerous taken in large quantities, was used for putting on bee and wasp stings, as an antidote for poisons, as a cure for dizziness and to take away warts and pimples.

Some herbal cures
Many of the herbal cures do now seem rather fanciful. The very few listed below are included for their interest value, you are not really advised to try them.

An eighteenth century Sussex remedy for ague—which was probably a fever—prescribes 'seven Sage leaves to be eaten by the patient fasting seven mornings running'.

Asthma sufferers, even as late as the first quarter of the twentieth century, were advised to 'mince Garlic, spread it on thin bread and butter, and eat just before going to bed'.

At the same time a dandruff cure, which unfortunately is not specific about the quantity of Sage in a packet, or how to dissolve it, recommended that you 'Take one packet and a half of Sage, and dissolve it in one pint of boiling water. When cold, strain into a bottle and brush into the scalp every night.' (If you do consider trying this be careful, the Sage liquid will stain walls and clothes, and may, like some hair-colourants, temporarily stain your scalp!)

Gout was a disease traditionally thought to result from rich-living and over-indulgence. But some of the cures for it had great simplicity, if not austerity. One late nineteenth-century remedy was that 'a clove of Garlic be eaten night and morning'.

An Australian hint, undated, for anyone troubled with their kidneys reads: 'Take a handful of Parsley, cover it with water and boil for a while. Strain and when cool drink a glassful.'

Two particularly odd herbal cures state

1591. THE RAPE OF HELEN BY PARIS: BY A FOLLOWER OF FRA ANGELICO ACTIVE 1417 – DIED 1455 ·

Elecampane is named after Helen of Troy (above). And one legend tells that the plant sprang from the tears she shed after being abducted by Paris.

Euphrosyne, whose name in Greek means gladness, was one of the Three Graces (left) and gave her name to Eyebright —Euphrasia Officinalis.

that to improve a bad memory you should drink Sage tea, sweetened to taste, and that Garlic sliced and worn in the socks will cure rheumatism.

To keep your skin clear some herbalists advise you to boil Elder flowers in water, strain, and then drink the liquid. And a nice seventeenth-century recipe for 'An excellent water for Ye sight' says: 'Take Fennel, Anniseed and Elecampane, dry and powder them, mix in good brandy, dry it again; Every morning and evening eate a pretty quantity, it is excellent for the sight.' While another of the same period tells you to 'Take good White Wine, infuse Eyebright in it three dayes, then Seethe it with a little Rosemary, drink it often, it is most excellent to restore and strengthen the sight. Also eate of the powder of Eyebright in a new laid egg rare-roasted every morning.'

A Welsh antidote for a spider's bite was to mix Garlic, treacle, and ale—unfortunately the quantities are not given. But you were supposed to drink freely of the mixture so ale probably predominated.

There are many complicated and expensive recipes for removing freckles and sunburn, mostly dating from the times when a pale skin was the sign of a lady. Rather more useful ones are those which tell you how to stop sunburn hurting. One such advises washing the affected part with Sage tea. Another says 'When the face and neck are sunburnt simmer two pounds of fresh Elder flowers in two pounds of hog's lard until crisp and then strain through sieve. Leave to cool and then apply the ointment to the burnt area.'

If you wanted to keep your teeth from rotting—an important concern in the days before dentures, fillings and toothpaste—you had to 'wash the mouth continually with the juice of Lemons and afterward rub your teeth with a Sage leaf, and wash your teeth after meat with fair water.'

Finally, a delightful recipe for 'Comforting the Head and the Braine' which says: 'Take Rosemary and Sage of both sorts of both, with flowers of Rosemary if to be had, and Borage with ye Flowers. Infuse in good Canary wine for three days, drink it often.' The wine certainly makes it sound a pleasant cure.

The medicinal herbs

The medicinal properties of herbs were second in importance only to the culinary qualities. Below are listed the traditional medicinal usages and beliefs attributed to various herbs—obviously not all the reputed curative properties are to be relied upon or tested.

Agrimony. This is an ancient medicinal herb. The Greeks used it to cure cataract. In Britain many centuries later it was made into a spring tonic and a blood purifier which was 'good for them that have naughty livers'.

Bergamot. Because, like all the Mints, it contains thymol, Bergamot used to be made into an infusion for colds and sore throats.

It is only quite recently that its qualities as a tea have been discovered in Europe, but they have been famous for centuries in the northern part of the United States, and in Canada. The Oswego Indians must have been the first to use its leaves to make a tea, for in North America this plant is named after them. After the 'Boston Tea Party', (December 16, 1773) patriotic American colonists drank it instead of Indian tea.

The Apothecary.

Its fragrance when it is growing make it a good bee plant and one of its American names is Bee Balm.

Borage. Even in Roman times, Borage had the reputation of being a cheerful, encouraging plant, one that, in Pliny's words, 'bring always courage'.

Centuries later, the great Elizabethan gardener and herbalist, John Gerard had the same praise for it in its use 'for the comfort of the heart, to drive away sorrow'. He—and many other people—had found that the effect of its leaves in a salad was 'to exilerate and make the mind glad', and the idea of an exhilarating salad is delicious in itself.

Borage was grown, too, for the beauty of its vivid blue flowers—Louis XIV had some planted in the gardens of Versailles—and they have been much copied in embroidery for centuries.

Catmint, Catnip. The true Catmint is *Nepeta cataria* which, said John Gerard, cats love so much that 'they rub themselves upon it, wallow or tumble in it, and also feed upon the branches and leaves very greedily.' People liked it very well too—as a medicine. It was regarded as 'a present helpe for them that be bursten inwardly of some fall received from a high place'. That makes it sound more a miracle than a medicine, but 'bursten inwardly' was just a vivid version of 'bruise'.

Chervil. This is yet another herb which the Romans brought into Europe from the shores of the Mediterranean and the Levant.

In England in the fifteenth century it was an essential plant, and it stayed in favour. For John Gerard, Chervil made salads that excelled 'in wholesomeness for the cold and feeble stomache'. The boiled roots were a preventive against plague. It could be eaten to cure the hiccups, and its leaves soothed the pain of rheumatism and bruises.

Chives. One of the most ancient of all herbs, Chives were a favourite in China as long ago as 3000 BC. They were enjoyed for their mild, delicious onion flavour, and used as an antidote to poison and to stop bleeding. For a herb, Chives came late to the gardens of Europe, arriving in the sixteenth century.

Coltsfoot. Its old country name, Son-before-Father, was given to it because the flowers appear before the leaves. For many centuries Coltsfoot (or Coughwort) flowers have been valued for their use in treating various lung complaints, particularly bronchitis and asthma. They were dried, and then inhaled or smoked, and have been used as a substitute for tobacco, too.

Comfrey. There is a tradition that Comfrey was much grown in the herb gardens of monasteries. That may have been because monks so often had to care for the sick and injured, and one of the old names for Comfrey was Knit-Bone.

It was believed to mend broken bones, and to heal such things as bruises, sprains, swellings and backache. One Elizabethan recipe is for Comfrey root, boiled in sugar and liquorice, and mixed with Coltsfoot, Mallow and Poppy seeds to make an ointment for curing bad backs and strains. But its use was not confined to muscular troubles, people also made Comfrey tea for colds and bronchitis, using an ounce of dried leaves to one pint of boiling water.

Dill. The common name comes from the Norse word *dilla*, meaning 'lull'—

Dill was believed to be good for insomnia. The seed is used in a mild medicine for flatulence, good for soothing a 'windy' baby.

Elecampane. The botanical name, *Inula Helenium*, comes from Helen of Troy. There is a legend that the plant sprang from her tears, but John Gerard says that her hands were full of it when Paris took her away from Greece.

Elecampane looks like a sunflower, and in Germany there was an ancient custom of putting a bunch of it in the centre of a nosegay of herbs to symbolize the sun and the head of Odin, the greatest of the Norse gods.

The Romans, in their practical way, used the roots in a medicine for the cure of over-eating, and Tudor herbalists candied them to use for the treatment of coughs, catarrahs, bronchitis, and chest ailments generally.

Eyebright. The botanical name, *Euphrasia Officinalis*, comes from Euphrosyne, one of the three Graces, whose name is the Greek word for gladness, and the common name comes from its use as an eye lotion. Milton, in *Paradise Lost*, speaks of how it was used with Rue to restore Adam's sight.

Long ago, country people used to use it, too, for an early morning drink, and in some places they made wine from it. In the North of England, where it grows on Hadrian's Wall, it was used to treat hay fever.

Fennel. The Greeks thought very highly of Fennel and used it for slimming and for treating more than twenty different illnesses. The Romans ate it—root, leaf and seed—in salads and baked it in bread and cakes. In Anglo-Saxon times it was used on fasting days, presumably because, as the Greeks had already discovered, it stilled the pangs of hunger. Even in later centuries it was 'much used in drink to make people more lean that are too fat'.

In the Middle Ages, Fennel was a favourite strewing herb for, apart from being fragrant, it kept insects at bay. It had a high place in the kitchen, too, lending its flavour to food that was often far from fresh to make it palatable. The royal household of Edward I, who reigned in England towards the end of the thirteenth century, used Fennel at the rate of 8½ pounds each month.

Fennel even had power against witches. If it were hung over the doorway on Midsummer Eve it would keep them away. And people who put it in the keyhole of their bedroom made sure that nothing dangerous would disturb their sleep.

Garlic. This is one of the oldest and most valued of all cultivated plants. It

DOCTOR BOKANKY, THE STREET HERBALIST.

[*From a Daguerreotype by* BEARD.]

"Now then for the Kalibonca Root, that was brought from Madras in the East Indies. It'll cure the toothache, head-ache, giddiness in the head, dimness of sight, rheumatics in the head, and is highly recommended for the ague; never known to fail; and I've sold it for this six and twenty year. From one penny to sixpence the packet. The best article in England."

may have come into Southern Europe from the East. Certainly it was known to the Ancient Egyptians who used it as a food and a medicine and thought so highly of it that it seemed almost a god to them. The builders of the pyramids ate it; the Children of Israel ate it; the Romans—needless to say—ate it and encouraged other people to do the same. It was an ingredient in medicine for leprosy—the term for a leper in the Middle Ages was pilgarlic, because he had to peel his own.

The antiseptic quality of Garlic is not just a matter of faith—in the First World War, sphagnum moss soaked in garlic juice was used for wound dressings. Garlic was valued in other medicines, too, for the digestion and for colds, coughs and asthma, And an old country remedy for whooping cough was to put a clove of Garlic in the shoes of the whooper!

Horehound. The Greeks thought highly of it and used it as an antispasmodic drug. It was an antidote, too, for the bite of a mad dog, and this, of course, is how it got its common name.

Lemon Balm. *Melissa Offiinalis*, the botanical name for this herb, comes from the Greek word for 'bee' and the Greeks believed that bees would never go away from a hive if it grew nearby. The hives were even rubbed with it to make the bees welcome.

Lemon Balm had valuable qualities for human beings, too. It soothed tension. It was a dressing for wounds, especially sword wounds, and in the Middle Ages it was believed that a sprig of Lemon Balm placed on an injury was enough to staunch the blood. It was good for the ears, toothache, and sickness during pregnancy. It was held to cure mad dog bites, skin eruptions and crooked necks. It prevented baldness. And when made into an amulet in a piece of linen or silk, it caused the women who wore it to be beloved and happy.

With all these powers to its credit, it is not surprising that the Ancient Greeks had believed that it promoted long life, and that a Prince Llewellyn of Glamorgan drank 'Melissa tea'—so he claimed—every day of the 108 years of his life.

Lovage. The Greeks used Lovage for a medicine and so did the Romans. It was they who brought it to Britain and spread it about Central Europe.

Lovage was grown all through the 'Dark Ages'. It is yet another of the almost-all-purpose medicines: it was taken for sore throats, quinsy, and for eye ailments; for indigestion and stomach-ache, and for getting rid of boils, spots and freckles. It was also added to baths, most probably as the earliest deodorant.

In Central Europe, when girls went to meet their lovers, they wore Lovage in a bag hanging round their necks, and perhaps it was its use as a perfume that led to Lovage being put into love potions which were guaranteed to awaken everlasting devotion.

Pennyroyal. The Romans gave Pennyroyal the name *Mentha Pulegium*, for it kept away fleas, and *pulex* is the Latin for flea. The great John Gerard called this Pudding Grass. In Tudor times it was gathered in London among the marshy parts of 'Miles end...poore women being plenty to sell it in London markets'.

Maybe the 'poore women' of Gerard's day found a ready market for it because it had so many uses. Gerard himself claimed that it would purify 'Corrupt water' on sea voyages, and that it would cure 'swimming in the head and the paines and giddiness thereof'. And in dried and powdered form it was made into medicine for coughs and colds.

Rocket. This must have been an early form of anaesthetic. The Romans—who sometimes sound like travelling herbalists in chariots—ate both the leaves and the seeds, and the Elizabethans were extremely partial to it, too. One herbalist recommended its being taken before a whipping, so that the pain would not be felt, and another praised its use against the biting of the shrew mouse 'and other venomous beasts'!

Sage. Sage was yet another traveller to Britain and Northern Europe in the Roman baggage train. Its Latin name, *Salvia*, means 'health', and from very early times people believed that it was a source of well-being, both physical and mental.

The Greeks used it to counteract all manner of afflictions, including ulcers, consumption, snake bites and grief. The Romans ate it. The Chinese at one time preferred Sage tea to tea tea, partly for its tonic properties. It was held to be good for the brain, the senses and the memory; it strengthened the sinews; it was good for palsy and cured stitches; it made a good gargle and mouthwash and kept the teeth white. And Gerard recommended its use in the brewing of ale!

Savory. Savory was grown in Egypt in ancient times, and used in love potions. The Romans liked it, too, but they used it in a spicy sauce. When it became at home in Europe, it was chiefly as a medicine, for cheering people up, for tired eyes, for ringing in the ears, for indigestion, for wasp and bee stings, and for other shocks to the system.

Tarragon. *Artemisia Dracunculus* is the botanical name and *Dracunculus* means, charmingly, little dragon. In ancient times, the mixed juices of Tarragon and Fennel made a favourite drink of the kings of India. In the reign of Henry VIII, the little dragon made its way into English gardens, and the diarist, John Evelyn described it as 'friendly to the head, heart, and liver'.

Wormwood. Its grand name first, according to tradition, was *Parthenis Absinthum*, but Artemis, the Greek goddess of chastity, had so much benefit from it that she gave it her name and it became *Artemisia Absinthum*. There is even more to its name, for its bitter taste is proverbial, and *Absinthum* means 'destitute of delight'.

Wormwood was well thought of as a medicine for a number of complaints. It was used to cure quinsy, prevent drunkenness, and heal the bites of rats and mice, and, mixed with wine, Rosemary, Blackthorn and Saffron, it had a reputation for keeping people in good health. Wormwood had its magical qualities, too. If it was hung beside the door, it kept away evil spirits. And, back in the everyday world, if it was added to ink, it stopped mice from eating old letters.

Yarrow. The botanical name of a herb very often tells much of its early history —or maybe its early legend. Yarrow got its botanical name, *Achillea Millefolium*, because it was the herb used by the Greek hero Achilles to heal his warriors in the Trojan War. An old country name for it is 'Soldiers' Woundwort', and it was chiefly famed and used for its healing qualities, probably in the form of an ointment. In infusions it was taken as a tonic and a cure for feverish colds. People did try it, too, as a cure for baldness.

A woodcut showing the stylized nature of early herbal illustrations.

WILD HERBS

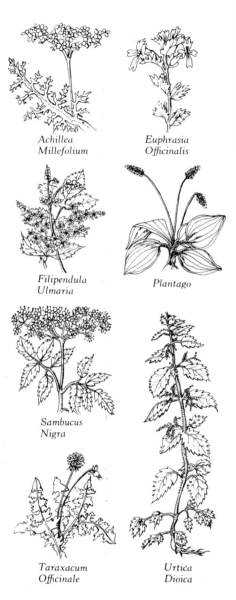

Achillea Millefolium

Euphrasia Officinalis

Filipendula Ulmaria

Plantago

Sambucus Nigra

Taraxacum Officinale

Urtica Dioica

Most good herbalists sell dried herbs from the wild places as well as the cultivated ones so a great deal is available. And if you grow a good mixture of herbs in your garden you will not need to track down herbs growing wild. It is a tempting and, perhaps, romantic thought to gather wild herbs in the early morning or—as recommended in so many old herbals—by the light of the new moon, but you must, obviously, know what you are doing, otherwise you may poison yourself.

So, first arm yourself with a good, fully-

illustrated reference book so that you know exactly what you are looking for and are sure you are picking the right thing. If you are in any doubt at all—do not pick it. It is, of course, almost impossible to go wrong with Dandelions, Nettles, Coltsfoot, Elder and Meadowsweet. It is when you are wondering which Eyebright and which Agrimony to pick and infuse that you might run into trouble.

Another important point to bear in mind is that nowadays, sadly, many wild plants are polluted in one way or another. So be careful that the hedgerow plants along leafy lanes are not covered with dust and noxious fumes from cars, and in the depths of the country make sure that no chemical spraying has been going on in the neighbourhood lately.

However, as so many people like to go out into the country and pick and use the flowers and berries that they find, here is a list of the easiest to come by and recognize.

Achillea Millefolium (Yarrow, Milfoil). A familiar hedgerow plant which grows to 1½-2 feet high and has flat white flowerheads. It is still used as a tea to ease severe colds and was traditionally used to staunch wounds.

Agrimonia Eupatoria (Agrimony, also known as Church Steeples). Agrimony is a perennial herb, has spikes of yellow flowers, and grows 1-2 feet high. From the time of the ancient Greeks it has been valued and esteemed for its medicinal properties, and Culpeper admired its sweet and fruity scent.

Euphrasia Officinalis (Eyebright). A tough little herb, growing 1-10 inches high with white or lilac flowers, Eyebright is found growing wild on downs and heaths, and in poor soil areas. It was traditionally used to cure eye disease—as its name would suggest.

Filipendula Ulmaria syn. *Spiraea Ulmaria* (Meadowsweet or Queen of the Meadows). This grows 2-4 feet high and has white flowers. In Tudor England it was loved and admired above any other wild plant, and was a favourite strewing herb of Elizabeth I. The leaves and flowers can be used to make a tea which is supposedly good for colds.

Plantago (Plantain). There are about 260 varieties of Plantain—mainly small plants under 6 inches high with tiny insignificant purple or white flowers. Unfortunately, although Plantain used to be prized as a herb with healing qualities it is now almost universally treated as a weed. Its freshly-picked leaves can, however, be used for a very good tea.

Sambucus nigra (Elder). Elder trees and bushes grow along hedges and in fields. The lacy flat flowers come out in early summer and the berries in early autumn. The flowers are picked and dried (face down) for Elderflower tea (see pages 22-23). And the leaves can also be cut into strips and boiled for tea when no flowers are available.

The Elder berries are often added to blackberries for jam and tarts. They are a favourite basis for a country wine which tastes rather like port.

Taraxacum Officinale (Dandelion). Dandelions are very nutritious and, with their distinctive small plants and yellow flowers, are easily recognizable. For recipes and uses of Dandelions see pages 20, 28 and remember that a tea made from either fresh or dried Dandelion leaves is good for all digestive upsets and rheumatic conditions.

Tilia Europaea (Lime). Flowers appear on the Lime tree in early summer and are much loved by bees. The flowers are dried to make one of the nicest teas or tisanes to drink last thing at night.

Tussilago Farfara (Coltsfoot). The small Coltsfoot with its yellow flowers grows everywhere, even on waste land in towns and cities. It is one of the oldest remedies for treating catarrh and chest troubles—in fact its latin name comes from *tussil*, cough; and was coined by Pliny to refer to the medicinal use of its leaves.

Urtica Dioica (Nettle). Most people instantly recognize and avoid the stinging Nettle. You can gather the young leaves and cook them as a vegetable or use them to make nettle beer. Nettle tea, too, has long been considered a good blood purifier.

which herbs with what

dictionary of herbs

Those marked 'wild' are only included in the wild herbs section, no growing instructions are given for them.

	Culinary	Medicinal	Bee Plants	Decorative	Used in Flower Arrangements	Ideal for Scented Gardens	Edgings	Can be Grown in Window Boxes
Agrimony (*Agrimonia Eupatoria*)	*	*						
Angelica (*Angelica Archangelica*)	*	*	*	*	*			
Basil (*Ocimum Basilicum*)	*	*				*		
Bay (*Laurus Nobilis*)	*							
Bergamot (*Monarda Didyma*)	*	*	*	*	*	*		
Borage (*Borago Officinalis*)	*	*	*	*	*			*
Camomile (*Anthemis Nobilis*)	*	*						
Catnip, Catmint (*Nepeta Cataria*)	*	*						*
Chervil (*Anthriscus Cerefolium*)	*	*						*
Chives (*Allium Schoenoprasum*)	*	*		*				
Coltsfoot (*Tussilago Farfara*)		*						
Comfrey (*Symphytum Officinale*)		*		*				
Coriander (*Coriandrum Sativum*)	*	*		*				
Dandelion (*Taraxacum Officinale*)	*	*						
Dill (*Anethum Graveolens*)	*	*		*				
Elder (*Sambucus Nigra*)	*	*						
Elecampane (*Inula Helenium*)		*		*	*			
Eyebright (*Euphrasia Officinalis*)		*						
Fennel (*Foeniculum Officinalis*)	*	*		*	*			*
Garlic (*Allium Sativum*)	*	*						
Good King Henry or Mercury (*Chenopodium Bonus-Henricus*)	*							
Horehound (*Marrubium Vulgare*)	*	*					*	
Hyssop (*Hyssopus Officinalis*)	*	*	*	*		*		
Lady's Mantle (*Alchemilla Vulgaris*)		*						
Lavender (*Lavandula Officinalis*)		*	*	*	*	*	*	*
Lemon Balm (*Melissa Officinalis*)	*	*	*					
Lemon Verbena (*Lippia Citriodora*)	*							
Lime (*Tilia Europaea*)	*			*				
Lovage (*Ligusticum Officinale*)	*	*	*					
Marigold (*Calendula Officinalis*)	*	*	*	*	*			
Marjorams (*Origanum sp.*)	*	*	*	*	*	*	*	*
Meadowsweet (*Spiraea Ulmaria*)		*	*	*	*			
Mints (*Mentha sp.*)	*	*		*			*	*
Mugwort (*Artemisia Vulgaris*)	*	*		*				
Nasturtium (*Tropaeolum Majus*)	*	*		*	*			*
Nettle (*Urtica Dioica*)	*							*
Parsley (*Carum Petroselinum*)	*							
Plantain (*Plantago*)	*							*
Purslane (*Portulaca Oleracea*)	*	*						
Rocket (*Eruca Sativa*)	*	*						
Rosemary (*Rosmarinus Officinalis*)	*	*	*	*	*	*	*	
Rue (*Ruta Graveolens*)		*		*			*	
Sage (*Salvia Officinalis*)	*	*	*	*			*	*
Salad Burnet (*Sanguisorba Minor*)	*	*						
Savory, Summer (*Satureja Hortensia*)	*	*	*	*			*	*
Savory, Winter (*Satureja Montana*)	*	*	*	*			*	*
Sorrel (*Rumex Acetosa*)	*	*						
Southernwood (*Artemisia Abrotanum*)				*				
Sunflower (*Helianthus Annuus*)	*	*	*	*	*			
Sweet Cicely (*Myrrhis Odorata*)	*	*	*	*	*			
Tarragon (*Artemisia Dracunculus*)	*							*
Thymes (*Thymus sp.*)	*	*	*	*		*		*
Vervain (*Verbena Officinalis*)	*					*		
Violet (*Viola Odorata*)	*	*				*		
Woodruff (*Asperula Odorata*)	*	*		*				
Wormwood (*Artemisia Absinthum*)		*		*				
Yarrow, Milfoil (*Achillea Millefolium*)	*	*						

Achillea Millefolium: Yarrow, Milfoil. (Wild)
Agrimonia Eupatoria: Agrimony (Wild)
Alchemilla Vulgaris: Lady's Mantle
Allium Sativum: Garlic
Allium Schoenoprasum: Chives
Anethum Graveolens: Dill
Angelica Archangelica: Angelica
Anthemis Nobilis: Camomile
Anthriscus Cerefolium: Chervil
Artemisia Abrotanum: Southernwood, also called Old Man, Lad's Love and Maiden's Ruin
Artemisia Absinthum: Wormwood
Artemisia Dracunculus: Tarragon
Artemisia Vulgaris: Mugwort
Asperula Odorata: Woodruff
Borago Officinalis: Borage
Calendula Officinalis: Marigold
Carum Petroselinum: Parsley
Chenopodium Bonus-Henricus: Good King Henry or Mercury
Coriandrum Sativum: Coriander
Eruca Sativa: Rocket
Euphrasia Officinalis: Eyebright (Wild)
Filipendula Ulmaria: Meadowsweet or Queen of the Meadows (Wild)
Foeniculum Vulgare: Fennel
Helianthus Annuus: Sunflower
Hyssopus Officinalis: Hyssop
Inula Helenium: Elecampane
Laurus Nobilis: Bay
Lavandula Officinalis: Lavender
Ligusticum Officinale: Lovage
Lippia Citriodora: Lemon Verbena
Marrubium Vulgare: Horehound
Melissa Officinalis: Lemon Balm
Mentha sp.: Mints
  Mentha Piperita: Peppermint
  Mentha Pulegium: Pennyroyal
  Mentha Rotundifolia: Round-leaved Mint
  Mentha Spicata syn. Mentha Viridis: Spearmint, Lamb Mint, Common Green Mint
Monarda Didyma: Bergamot, Bee Balm, Oswego Tea
Myrrhis Odorata: Sweet Cicely
Nepeta Cataria: Catmint, Catnip
Ocimum Basilicum: Basil
Origanum sp.: Marjoram
  Origanum Majorana syn. Majorana Hortensis: Oregano or Knotted Marjoram
  Origanum Onites: French Marjoram
  Origanum Vulgare: Pot Marjoram
Plantago: Plantain (Wild)
Portulaca Oleracea: Purslane
Rosmarinus Officinalis: Rosemary
Rumex Acetosa: Sorrel
Ruta Graveolens: Rue
Salvia Officinalis: Sage
Sambucus Nigra: Elder (Wild)
Sanguisorba Minor syn. Poterium: Salad Burnet
Satureja: Savory
  Satureja Hortensis: Summer Savory
  Satureja Montana: Winter Savory
Symphytum Officinale: Comfrey, also known as Knit-bone and Boneset
Taraxacum Officinale: Dandelion (Wild)
Thymus sp.: Thymes
  Thymus Vulgaris: Common Thyme
  Thymus Citriodorus: Lemon Thyme
Tilia Europaea: Lime (Wild)
Tropaeolum Majus: Nasturtium
Tussilago Farfara: Coltsfoot (Wild)
Urtica Dioica: Nettle (Wild)
Verbena Officinalis: Vervain
Viola Odorata: Violet, sweet

Bay　Fennel　Lovage　Elder

Dill　Parsley　Rosemary

Sage

Marjoram

Sorrel　Savory　Chervil

Thyme

Basil

Chives

Mints and Tarragon

Chives

Hedge of Roses
Stachys Lanata

Bay　Rue　Catmint

Catmint　Rue　Lovage

Parsley

Mints and Tarragon

Artemisia

Chervil

Pinks

Marjoram

Pinks

Lavender

Rose and Thyme

Lavender

Chives　Pinks

Pinks　Chives

Sage

Artemisia

Artemisia　Sage

Parsley

Angelica

Basil　Chives

Chives　Fennel

Lavender

Lavender